Lang.

BRITISH FOREIGN POLICY
IN THE INTER-WAR YEARS

BRITISH
FOREIGN POLICY
in the
INTER-WAR YEARS

BY

P. A. REYNOLDS

LONGMANS, GREEN AND CO
LONDON . NEW YORK · TORONTO

LONGMANS, GREEN AND CO LTD
6 & 7 CLIFFORD STREET LONDON W I
ALSO AT MELBOURNE AND CAPE TOWN

LONGMANS, GREEN AND CO INC
55 FIFTH AVENUE NEW YORK 3

LONGMANS, GREEN AND CO
215 VICTORIA STREET TORONTO I

ORIENT LONGMANS LTD
BOMBAY CALCUTTA MADRAS

First published 1954

Printed in Great Britain by
Latimer, Trend & Co Ltd, Plymouth

PREFACE

THIS SHORT SURVEY of British inter-war foreign policy was originally written for publication in Germany, where twelve years of Nazi control of opinion and writing, together with the physical devastation of the Second World War, had largely destroyed the foundations upon which study of twentieth-century history could be built. Being intended as an introduction to the subject for use in the upper forms of schools and in the early years at a university, the book did not claim to present any new interpretation or to be based on profound and long research. Its material was drawn from a fairly wide range of secondary sources, together with some supplementation from League of Nations records, from the *Documents on British Foreign Policy, 1919-1939* now being published under the editorship of Professor Sir Llewelyn Woodward and Mr. Rohan Butler, from the *Documents on German Foreign Policy, 1918-1945* in process of publication under joint American, British and French editorship, and from special documentary collections such as the *Proceedings of the International Military Tribunal at Nuremberg*, and *Ciano's Diplomatic Papers*, edited by Malcolm Muggeridge. Occasional use was made of Press sources, and the evidence of varying reliability from the large mass of memoirs, British, French, American and German, was extensively called in aid. The present English edition has been prepared as a result of private suggestions that the book might meet a need in this country: the original text has been in some places revised in order to take account of recently published documentary evidence. The intention has been to present as accurate a record as possible, with the materials available, and in brief compass, of the course of British policies in the inter-war period, and of the factors underlying those policies.

It must be recognized that the "materials available" for a study of this kind are both too many and too few. The twentieth-

Preface

century historian has a far greater mass of evidence than any of his fellows working in earlier fields: this is primarily due to the developing complexity of inter-state relations political, economic, strategic and cultural through the last century and a half, resulting from scientific and technological advances that have thrown all parts of the world into ever closer contact. All major governments now necessarily maintain large expert staffs to deal with foreign relations, and expansion of staffs itself demands increased interchange of information, and therefore increased documentation. The process received a great impetus with the introduction of the telegraph in the mid-nineteenth century, making possible far more rapid intercommunication, report and instruction. The wealth of material is further multiplied by the extension of governmental activity in economic and strategic matters with a greater or less bearing on the evolution of foreign relations. And beyond the problem of bulk is the problem of technicality: a large proportion of diplomatic documents now consist of expert memoranda and reports on political, economic, social, ethnographical, and above all defence questions that require a considerable degree of expert or technical knowledge for their proper understanding.

On the other hand materials are too few. Governments are naturally cautious about the revelations they permit of the inner workings of recent policies, for reasons of security, for fear of the effect of such revelations on current international relations, or because other governments and living persons are likely to be concerned. The United States government is the most generous in this regard, that of the Soviet Union the most secretive. Despite the quantity of material, then, it is almost always incomplete, and occasionally there are serious gaps. The Abyssinian crisis, for example, one of the three decisive issues in the inter-war years, has as yet little reliable documentation. These gaps can be filled only by cautious and painstaking study of parliamentary and Press reports, and of memoirs, where such exist, on the model of Professor Sir Lewis Namier's masterly *Diplomatic Prelude*; but conclusions reached on the basis of sources such as these must remain tentative and open to revision in the light of later evidence.

Nevertheless, within the limits imposed by the paucity and the richness of the sources, historical methods can be applied

vi

no less than to the study of the Middle Ages or the seventeenth century. As the subject of study approaches closer to the present, it becomes progressively more difficult to exclude the influence of present knowledge, but the writer must keep constantly in his mind the effect of such influence on his selection of evidence and subject. No less must the reader endeavour to banish any awareness of present conditions that leads him to find in the printed word a meaning that it will not bear in any save its proper historical context.

P. A. R.

Aberystwyth
1953

MAPS

CONTENTS

TABLE OF DATES

Chapter 1

THE UNITED KINGDOM AFTER
THE FIRST WORLD WAR

THE UNITED KINGDOM emerged from the 1914-18 war a gravely weakened power. Her loss of relative strength was due partly to the effects of the war itself, political, economic and strategic, and partly to the emergence of many new "middle-power" states whose existence alone would have lessened the great powers' mastery of affairs even had they not been weakened or destroyed by the war. This dominant position of the great powers[1] during the nineteenth century had been due partly to their great and increasing populations (in 1914 only the Ottoman Empire, Spain and Abyssinia outside the ranks of the great powers had populations over ten million, with the exception of China which at that date was not a unified country under a single administration);[2] partly to the tradition of the Concert of Europe, through which (as for example in 1878 or 1912) the great powers of Europe met together to regulate by agreement among themselves contentious international problems; partly to the development of the science of war, the cost of armaments, and the practice of conscription, all of which made military strength dependent on population, natural resources and financial power; but most of all to the industrial revolution which, by its transformation of productive capacity, of communications and of social relationships, both encouraged the formation of larger and more efficient political units (such as Germany and Italy), and enabled those units more effectively to mobilize their much greater resources. Great Britain had been the first country to undergo the industrial revolution, with its concomitant increase of population, and this—together with her maritime supremacy and her world-wide connections,

---

[1] Great Britain, France, Germany, Italy, Russia, Austria-Hungary, the United States and, at the end of the century, Japan.

[2] Toynbee, A. J., *The World After the Peace Conference*, p. 12. O.U.P., 1926.

I

her long period of internal tranquillity and her longer immunity from invasion—had enabled her to amass great wealth, and establish a long lead in the race for industrial and economic development and expansion. In the early stages of this advance she had played a major part in the defeat of Napoleon, and her representative, Castlereagh, had been able to speak with authority both in the making of the Vienna settlement and in the creation of the Concert of Europe.

This pre-eminence of Britain among the powers was already being challenged before the outbreak of the First World War. The newly unified Germany had established a dominant position in Europe by her defeat of France in 1870, and by 1914 her influence was reaching out into the Middle East, Africa and the Far East, and was even making itself felt on the seas, the most essential and jealously guarded sector of Britain's defence and power. Furthermore, and more significantly, by 1913 Germany had exceeded Britain's total volume of manufactures (though not her manufactured exports).[1] Already twenty years earlier Great Britain's production of manufactures had been surpassed by the United States;[2] and by the turn of the century Japan was emerging as a potentially formidable economic competitor, after her incredibly rapid transformation into a modern industrial state in the course of a single generation. Moreover, the greater size and resources of the United States and Germany, and the very fact that their major industrialization had been later and had therefore made use of more up-to-date methods and equipment, spelled a further threat to Britain's position of world economic leadership—indeed in the long run possibly threatened even her standard of life and her economic stability.

These pre-war economic trends were greatly accelerated by the war, and were reinforced by other factors, political and strategic, that undermined the position of the United Kingdom. In the first place, the Concert of Europe (which had maintained something of an international tradition, and in which Britain had at times exercised her influence) was shattered: of the 1914 great powers Germany was defeated and disarmed, Russia was

---

[1] Robinson, E. A. G., in *United Kingdom Policy, Foreign, Strategic and Economic*, p. 60. R.I.I.A., 1950.
[2] *Ibid.*

in chaos, Austria-Hungary had disintegrated, France was exhausted and embittered, Italy dissatisfied. None was able or willing to pursue those policies of conciliation and co-operation which Britain above all needed in view of her dependence for economic recovery on a high level of world trade. Only Britain, in the first five years after 1918, retained anything of such spirit of international conciliation as had existed among European powers before 1914, a spirit in which she had been able to exercise some influence in favour of peace, her prime national interest.

But a more striking weakening of Britain's political position derived from the change in the nature of her relations with the other countries of the Commonwealth. The enhanced status of the Dominions was signalized by their appearance at the peace conference of Paris as fully independent states (although this status was not wholly formalized until the passing of the Statute of Westminster in 1931), and the necessity of acting on major issues in accord with six[1] other sovereign states often delayed and at times gravely embarrassed United Kingdom action in the international field. The United Kingdom's lessened economic and strategic independence as a result of the war further increased the importance of co-ordinating policies with the Dominions.

A more serious weakening in Britain's political position, however, resulted from the influence of the war on "colonial and semi-colonial" peoples. The closeness and magnitude of the struggle had demanded the mobilization of all resources in all parts of the world, the universal introduction of conscription, and the imposition of blockade and counter-blockade. Measures such as these affected every member of every nation, and in order to persuade peoples of the need to endure them, war aims were reformulated in phrases with a popular appeal. The war was to make the world safe for democracy, it was a war to end war, and the post-war policy of the Allies would be based on the right of self-determination. Various measures were taken to forward these aims in the latter part of the war itself. As the largest world colonial power, Britain was chiefly exposed to the

---

[1] Effectively with four—Canada, Australia, New Zealand and South Africa—for neither the Irish Free State nor Newfoundland normally played any great part in Commonwealth consultation.

dangers presented by the aspirations to which these slogans had given rise: thus in the vital region of the Middle East (a major interest for the United Kingdom as a means of communication with the East, as a source of oil, and as a barrier against Russian southward expansion) Britain had at one and the same time encouraged nationalist aspirations among the Arabs against Turkey and stimulated Zionist hopes for a National Home in Palestine, and had thus herself created elements of conflict and undermined her own position in a key area; in India nationalist stirrings towards independence had received great stimulus both from the experiences of Indians during the war and from the ideas then fostered; in the Far East Britain's interests faced a twofold threat, from the imperialist expansionism of Japan foreshadowed in the Twenty-one Demands on China in 1915, and from the nascent nationalism of China herself which had already overthrown the Manchu dynasty in 1911 and which was to lead to the Kuomintang movement against foreign privileges in the middle 'twenties. Finally, within the frontiers of the United Kingdom the influence of a wider public opinion—driven by the horrors of war to pay attention to international affairs—was to be of as yet incalculable effect on the weakness or strength of particular governments on particular occasions.

Britain's power was undermined strategically no less than politically. Technological developments before and during the war had lessened the measure of security that the Channel had conferred on Britain ever since she began to assert her strength on the seas in the sixteenth century. The industrial revolution had been the path to Britain's greatness in the nineteenth century, but it had also brought her into dependence for economic survival on imported food for her expanded population and imported raw materials for her industries. The safeguarding of maritime communications had therefore become vital to Britain's very existence, and the development of the submarine presented a new military threat that had barely been countered in time in 1917. Just as there was new danger below the water, so there was new potential danger above it; for although by 1918 aircraft had not been sufficiently developed to present a major threat to the British Isles, the Channel could no longer be expected to provide so complete a degree of security against military devastation or invasion as before 1914. To put it at its

4

very lowest, the strategic problem demanded the provision of an air power strong enough to counter any airborne threat over the Channel, and the need to maintain a strong air force as well as a powerful navy seriously increased the economic burden of defence.

Politically, then, Britain's world position was shaken, strategically it was to some extent undermined. But it was in the acceleration of pre-war economic trends that the war had its gravest effects on the strength of the United Kingdom. Productivity per head of the population declined through death or injury among the most productive age-groups, through insufficient replacement of capital goods and over-driving of machinery, through over-cultivation of land with uneconomic or insufficient rotation of crops; the diversion of industrial activity to war production and the imposition of blockades prevented the supplying of pre-war export markets and caused importing countries either to buy elsewhere or to establish their own industries; invisible export income was seriously reduced by the expansion of the United States mercantile marine in the face of British merchant-shipping losses, by the sale of overseas investments, and by the rise of prices, which decreased the purchasing power of such investments as remained; perhaps most important, the stimulus given by the war to United States production, the demands on her for manufactured goods, her capture of markets that Britain and Europe could no longer supply, her transformation from a debtor to a creditor nation— all these factors together with her great natural wealth and expanding population placed the United States in a position of rival and potential master of Great Britain in her fields of traditional supremacy, now vital to her existence, those of finance and commerce. The process by which the commercial and financial supremacy of the United States was established was indeed completed only by the Second World War, but by 1918 the United Kingdom had lost that practical monopoly of many markets which had been the foundation of her great prosperity. These economic factors operated, of course, to a greater or less degree for all the European industrial countries, and all were weaker thereby. It is also true that the war caused greater immediate suffering to countries other than Britain—to France and Belgium by the devastation of their richest areas, to Germany by her defeat and its aftermath, to Russia by revolution and civil war. But the cumulative long-term effects of the war may well have been greatest on Great Britain, first because of her new strategic requirements, secondly because of the complexities of her political position in the Commonwealth on the maintenance of which any remaining measure of power must depend, thirdly because of the exposure of her world-wide interests to the new forces roused or stimulated by the war, and fourthly because of the weakening in her economic position which was common to all the manufacturing countries of Europe, but which more seriously affected the United Kingdom in view of the degree of her dependence on overseas income and the sale of her goods to pay for her food and raw materials.

The basic foreign policies of Great Britain since the period of civil conflict in the middle of the seventeenth century have been primarily determined by her geographical situation as a small island lying off the coast of a continent of powerful peoples, dependent for such strength as she had on the development and exploitation of overseas connections and interests in India and the New World, and at a later date in Africa and the Far East. Her two major endeavours in the field of foreign policy have therefore been the maintenance of command of the seas, whether by herself alone or in alliance with some other naval power or powers; and the prevention of mastery of the European continent by any one great power. The former policy served the two ends of ensuring the safety of the British Isles from invasion, and of protecting the colonies, outposts and bases, and the commercial and strategic routes to them, upon which Britain's prosperity and power so largely depended. The part that foreign policy had to play in maintaining command of the seas (ultimately a naval and strategic problem) was to prevent any grouping of naval powers that could threaten Britain's vital interests or communications in any part of the world; and with the development of naval power and of its cost, and with the extension of Britain's world commitments, this task became progressively greater. Thus by 1914 Britain had abandoned control of the Caribbean to the United States, of Far Eastern waters to Japan, and of the Mediterranean to France,[1] and had

---

[1] Webster, C. K., in *United Kingdom Policy, Foreign, Strategic and Economic*, p. 14.

therefore become largely dependent on the maintenance of good relations with those countries, unless equally effective substitutes capable of serving the same purposes could be found.

Just as the guarding of the Channel and of overseas communications was vital to the maintenance of Britain's strength, so her evident interest lay in preventing the mastery of the continent of Europe by any one power, which could then mobilize all the resources of the Continent against her and kill the Empire by destroying its heart. This factor entered into almost all the major wars fought by Great Britain—against Philip II of Spain, against Louis XIV and Napoleon of France, against imperial Germany and Hitler—and it remained a consistent principle of policy apart from occasional aberrations like the association of the restored Stuarts with France before their overthrow in 1688. Britain was, of course, never able to defeat such threats unaided (though she has often been the last resisting power behind her Channel rampart): her expedient was always to enter into alliance with one or more powers to defeat the conqueror. Not infrequently, after the successful issue of a conflict, she found herself compelled to turn against her former allies, whose ambitions in the flush of victory tempted them towards that very continental hegemony which Britain had but lately fought to prevent.[1]

These two, then, were the basic elements of British policy before 1914. In the broadest view, of course, the maintenance of peace must be the major interest of a commercial power dependent on a high level of world trade, and, in general, British influence was cast on the side of peace in the nineteenth century: up to the outbreak of the First World War she had refused to commit herself to any alliance involving mutual assistance, with the exception of that with Japan in 1902, in which the circumstances of assistance were narrowly defined. Among other elements of British policy the defence of democracy or the promotion of the cause of constitutionalism has often been adduced; but only on rare occasions is there evidence of this kind of ideological motivation for British action before 1914 when other and more cogent forces were not in operation.

---

[1] Attempts at hegemony after the defeat of a would-be conqueror were not always due to ambition backed by strength: the French attempt after 1918 was due much more to weakness and fear.

What, then, was the effect of Britain's weakened world position on these traditional policies, and how far were they modified? In general the effect was to intensify them, to increase Britain's concern with, and dependence on, the Commonwealth (and now on the United States), and to give added urgency to her endeavours to create and maintain a harmonious balance on the continent of Europe. The importance of relations with the United States was illustrated by the fate of the Anglo-Japanese alliance in 1921; the influence of Commonwealth ties was most strikingly evident in the attitude of the United Kingdom to the various French proposals for security in Europe in the 'twenties; British concern for peace found expression in the pursuit of disarmament; and her desire for peaceful regulation of Europe's problems caused her policy towards Germany to diverge widely from that of France from 1919 onwards.

The implementation of these policies in the inter-war years will be described in the following chapters, but a consideration of the position of the United Kingdom after the First World War cannot be complete without some discussion of her attitude towards the League of Nations. The need for some form of international organization after the war was widely recognized among leading thinkers in all the Allied countries, particularly in both the Democratic and the Republican parties in the United States. The war had shown not merely that international conflict with the weapons produced by twentieth-century scientific and technological skills was far more horrible and destructive than in earlier times: it had also demonstrated that the world was now a unity, both economically (instanced by the effect of conflict in one part of the world on the economy of others, and by the hardships imposed by the interruption of normal trade), and strategically (no major country was able to stand aside from the struggle). Furthermore, there was evident need for some substitute for the old European Concert which had been shattered by the war, and the idea of world organization for peace had an enormous appeal to those peoples who had suffered in the conflict.

The initial steps towards drafting a constitution for an international organization were taken by the British Commonwealth. While the League to Enforce Peace, with the powerful support of ex-President Taft, Senator Henry Cabot Lodge and, after mid-1916, President Wilson, had been preparing public opinion in the United States since 1915, the House Memorandum of 16 July 1918 on which Wilson's first draft of the Covenant was based, had itself made extensive use of the report of the Phillimore committee in the United Kingdom, drawn up in March. General Smuts (a member of the British War Cabinet) and a Foreign Office team under Lord Robert Cecil were already working on draft proposals, and these were largely amalgamated with Wilson's first draft in December 1918. Two further drafts by Wilson in January 1919 were combined with new British proposals by the British and United States legal advisers, Mr. (now Sir) Cecil Hurst and David Hunter Miller, and their draft of 2 February 1919 was that presented to the League commission of the plenary peace conference at Paris.

Already in the autumn of 1916 a Foreign Office memorandum had mentioned the possibility of some form of international organization after the war, and from Lloyd George's extensive quotations from this memorandum[1] it seems clear that its authors viewed the creation of such an organization with favour partly in order to make world disarmament possible, but primarily because the maintenance of international law and order required some international authority, just as internal order could be preserved only by the power of government. There was, however, little disposition in political, official or intellectual circles for any form of federation or world government involving ultimate abandonment of sovereignty in the fields of foreign affairs and defence, and the ways in which an international organization could contribute to the maintenance of peace—its prime object—were therefore restricted. Means suggested were the provision of machinery through which disputes could be discussed and settled peacefully; secondly, the laying of obligations on members of the organization to act together against a state deliberately resorting to war, thus making such a breach of the peace less likely; and thirdly the creation of economic, social and legal organs through which some of the underlying causes of conflict could be diminished or removed through international co-operation. But the object was the maintenance of peace, and if war nevertheless broke out, the

[1] Lloyd George, D., *The Truth about the Peace Treaties*, Vol. I, pp. 31-50. Gollancz, 1938.

organization would have failed in its primary task. This view of the League as an organ for the peaceful settlement of international disputes (and therefore on occasion for alterations in international agreements) was basically different from the French conception. A French draft for the constitution of an international organization laid before, but not considered in detail by, the League commission of the plenary conference at Paris, envisaged a permanent alliance of the Allied victors with an international armed force and an international general staff to prevent a renewed German attempt at European conquest. This initial conception was soon modified, so that by 1925 the French were pressing for a German entry into the League; but the French emphasis was always laid on the collective security aspect of the League's functions, on the organization of action against an aggressor (and, of course, the potential aggressor the French not unnaturally had constantly in mind was a resurgent Germany), and on Article 10 which declared the principles of territorial integrity and independence of members of the League. This difference of emphasis on the functions and methods of the League was among the most fundamental causes of dispute between Britain and France in the inter-war period: peaceful regulation of disputes and satisfaction of legitimate grievances rather than co-operation against attempted forcible redress, underlay the whole approach to international affairs of the primarily Conservative governments in Britain between 1919 and 1939. The view was well expressed by Austen Chamberlain in his speech of rejection of the Geneva Protocol before the League Council on 12 March 1925: "The fresh emphasis laid upon sanctions, the new occasions discovered for their employment, the elaboration of military procedure, insensibly suggest the idea that the vital business of the League is not so much to promote friendly co-operation and reasoned harmony in the management of international affairs as to preserve peace by organising war . . .";[1] and the same idea was again formulated in strikingly similar terms by his step-brother in the House of Commons on 24 March 1938 in answer to Litvinov's proposal for consultation on the practical measures called for by Nazi expansionism as revealed in the Austrian Anschluss: "Their [the Russian] proposal would appear to involve less a consulta-

[1] League of Nations *Official Journal*, 6th Year, No. 4: xxxiii Cl., p. 448.

tion with a view to settlement than a concerting of action against an eventuality that has not yet arisen",[1] or as the official Foreign Office reply put it: "A conference . . . designed less to secure the settlement of outstanding problems than to organise concerted action against aggression, would not necessarily . . . have such a favourable effect upon the prospects of European peace."[2] The unwillingness to enter a *bloc* against aggression persisted even into 1939, and was one of the factors that bedevilled the early stages of the Anglo-French negotiations with the Soviet Union. The Labour party placed far more emphasis on collective security, but they had accepted the cause of international organization after early suspicion towards it primarily as a means of forwarding their cherished project of peace through disarmament, and they therefore viewed collective security first and foremost as a means of preserving peace not as a means of organizing war. Their resolutions often coupled collective security with disarmament,[3] and they persisted into the latter 'thirties in refusing to support rearmament behind any but a collective security policy, thus appearing simultaneously as champions of the League and opponents of rearmament. This attitude played a major part in the confusion of British public opinion in the 'thirties, which enabled both parties to claim its support: in general, public opinion believed in, and wished to support a policy of collective security, and simultaneously opposed alliance with France, opposed rearmament, and favoured a settlement of Germany's "legitimate grievances". The policy of France and the character of the German government after 1933 made even more irreconcilable views which themselves were basically inconsistent.

The traditional nineteenth-century aims of British foreign policy then—the maintenance of command of the seas by means of her own naval strength supported by friendly relations with

[1] *Parly. Debs.*, Fifth Series H. of C., vol. 333, col. 1406.
[2] Woodward, E. L. and Butler, R., *Documents on British Foreign Policy, 1919-1939*, Third Series, Vol. I, p. 101. H.M.S.O., 1949.
[3] For example on 10 November 1932: "That . . . the British Government should give clear and unequivocal support to an immediate, universal, and substantial reduction of armaments on the basis of equality of status for all nations, and should maintain the principles of the covenant of the League of Nations by supporting the findings of the Lytton Commission on the Sino-Japanese dispute." *Parly. Debs.*, Fifth Series H. of C., Vol. 270, col. 525.

certain other naval powers, the promotion of a high level of world trade, the prevention of control of the continent of Europe by any one power, the preservation of peace—remained the guiding principles of British governments after 1918. The effects of the war on the political, strategic and economic position of the United Kingdom determined the broad lines of the policies these principles required. In the first place, the United Kingdom's main interests were necessarily centred on extra-European affairs to an even greater extent than before 1914. Closer relations with, and more deference to, the Dominions were dictated by their political advance, by the enormous burden of defence of global interests in the twentieth century, and by the United Kingdom's relative loss of economic strength. New threats to her position and interests in the Middle East, India and the Far East developed as a result of the war and of the post-war activities of the Bolsheviks. The enormous industrial expansion of the United States and her ability, should she so desire, to outmatch the British on the seas, forced the United Kingdom to align herself with American policies in the Pacific, and to pay a not unwilling heed to the attitude of the United States towards such international problems as disarmament.

In the second place, and as a corollary to the first, the United Kingdom's aims in Europe were to remove the grounds for disputes or peacefully resolve them, to avoid wide commitments that might involve too great an allocation of her extended resources, and to promote the economic restoration of Europe as part of her own economic recovery. The pursuit of these aims, which involved the political conciliation and the economic revival of Germany, necessarily caused British policies to diverge from those of France who, twice invaded and devastated by Germany, and aware of her weakness relative to the potential power of a revived Germany, endeavoured to maintain in their entirety the restrictions imposed by the Versailles treaty. Perhaps the central tragedy of the inter-war years lay in the ascendancy of French policies towards Germany when the latter's co-operation might still have been achieved, and in the prevailing of the British view when the German government was such that any attempt at co-operation was necessarily disastrous.

Finally, Britain's attitude to the League reflected the same fundamental principles. The League was a valuable organ for the canalization and settlement of international disputes, for the promotion of economic recovery and social co-operation, and for the preservation of an international balance; but it was a world-wide organization whose operation was not confined to European problems, and therefore commitments involving possible military action that a power with world interests such as Britain could assume must necessarily be more narrowly defined than those that could be undertaken by countries whose interests and fears were more concentrated in one part of the world, such as France. For this reason, attempts to insert automatic obligations in the Covenant were resisted by the United Kingdom (in the same way as she kept herself free from pacts involving mutual assistance), for her extra-European associates were unwilling to see her either too closely committed in European problems or too closely linked with an apparently intransigent France pursuing what appeared to be an unwise and unco-operative policy. Moreover, she well knew that her resources were no longer great enough to enable her to promise military or naval action in all parts of the world—action the burden of which, in the absence from the League of the United States, would inevitably fall upon her. The action that she took in any question that came before the League therefore depended on her internal and external situation at the time, and on the degree to which the matter in question affected her own vital interests; the same considerations guided the policy of the other leading member of the League, France, but since French interest in the League was centred on the single issue of Germany, her policy had an element of consistency that the British apparently lacked. André Tardieu could with apparent justice[1] counter Paul Reynaud's appeal for support to the British policy of collective security and sanctions against France's new friend, Italy, in 1935 by pointing to Britain's sabotage of the cause of collective security in 1925, when she turned down the Geneva Protocol, and in 1932-3 when she rejected the Paul-Boncour plan for disarmament with security. The most disastrous feature of British policy in the inter-war years was the rigidity

---

[1] In a letter resigning from the Republican Centre Party at the end of 1935, quoted in *Bulletin of International News*, R.I.I.A., Vol. XII, No. 13, p. 25. See Chapter 9, p. 118.

with which an understandable policy of caution towards widely conceived collective security in the 'twenties was pursued and intensified in the 'thirties (with the half-hearted exception of 1935) to the point of surrender of one of her traditional aims— the prevention of mastery of the Continent by a single power.

Chapter 2

SECURITY AND DISARMAMENT

THE PREVIOUS CHAPTER indicated in outline some of the fundamental divergencies between Britain and France in the inter-war years. The underground suspicion, distrust and antagonism between British and French policies—one of the keys to an understanding of the whole history of international relations between 1919 and 1939—was most strikingly evident in the Middle East (the subject of a later chapter) and in the problems of reparations, security and disarmament. These last three questions, with two of which this chapter deals, were merely different facets of a single problem—Germany.

For France the basic issues in the immediate post-war world were primarily political in character—how to prevent the, as she saw it, retrograde hegemony in Europe of a Germany whose potential economic and military strength (deriving from her great economic resources and her large and expanding population) was continually increasing relative to her own. Her potential relative weakness at a time of apparent great strength was never far from the minds of her leading statesmen, although they did not all agree on the methods by which the danger should be met. The collapse into chaos of France's 1914 ally in the east sharpened the sense of weakness; and the invasion and devastation of the north-eastern industrial territories during the 1914-18 war as a result of Germany's superior power were never long forgotten. For France, therefore, her own security (by which she meant the maintenance of the Versailles settlement) must be assured before she could contemplate any major measures of disarmament: some artificial means was necessary to prevent a German hegemony and its known consequences, therefore she must maintain an artificial armament disparity until her security was guaranteed. Once all nations felt secure, she argued, fear would be removed and thus disarmament would be made possible.

For Britain, on the other hand, the basic issues in the post-war world were economic, not political—how to restore world prosperity and world trade, and thus produce economic recovery in

Britain, reduce the burden of unemployment and raise the standard of living. Without a high level of world trade Britain's power and prosperity must decline; and Britain's statesmen and economists with increasing frequency and emphasis demonstrated how European and world recovery could make no more than limited advances while Germany remained a vast centre of economic depression. Britain's interests and policy therefore soon came to favour and require economic recovery in Germany: she could afford to look with equanimity upon some revival of Germany's power, because she had no war experiences equivalent to those of France, because she had considerable potential strength in association with the Commonwealth, and because of her inherited sense of security through the existence of the Channel and the power of her navy—a security increased in 1919 by the destruction of the German fleet. Great Britain, then, was averse from accepting any further political or military commitments in Europe (her interests were world-wide, not even primarily European), but strongly favoured the cause of disarmament, not merely as a step on the road to peace, but also as a means of reducing the economic burden of defence. Reduction of arms, British statesmen argued, would improve economic conditions, would thereby reduce international tension, and thus would create security. Disarmament must precede security, not the other way round.

These two interlocking problems appeared in the earliest stages of post-armistice discussions. On 25 February 1919 France demanded that the river Rhine should be the French frontier and that the bridges over the Rhine should be occupied by inter-Allied forces. These demands reflected the views of French military experts, headed by Marshal Foch, that the Rhine was the only effective strategic barrier to the advance of German or barbaric Bolshevik forces, that only through demilitarization of the Rhine could France bring swift aid to any of the new east European states should they be threatened by Germany or Russia, and that the foundation of any future German aggressive action against France could be destroyed only by occupation of the left bank of the Rhine and mastery of the strategic railway network in that region. Both Wilson and Lloyd George opposed the French demand—Wilson because it ran counter to the principle of self-determination and would

create a serious German grievance which could only be ground
for future war; Lloyd George because, in line with traditional
British policies, he wanted no one major European power to
dominate the Rhine and with it Belgium, and because he was
unwilling to saddle himself with a permanent or lengthy Allied
occupation, since large military establishments are economically
wasteful, and he had promised rapid demobilization. Accordingly, after intensive negotiations, Wilson and Lloyd George
successfully persuaded Clemenceau to agree that occupation of
the left bank should be a temporary measure as a reparations
guarantee. In return, they offered France a joint guarantee
against direct German aggression. On 28 March a Note from
the United States delegation formalized one part of the Rhine
frontier settlement (Germany was to build no fortifications, and
conduct no troop movements, in the occupied zone or in a strip
of territory along the right bank of the Rhine fifty kilometres
wide; violation of this provision would be considered a hostile
act against France; the United States pledged herself to assist
France against German aggression); and on 14 April, while
Lloyd George was away in London, Wilson, who had been
impressed by the French need for security, modified the compromise of 14 March by agreeing that the occupied zone on the
left bank of the Rhine should be divided into three areas, the
first to be evacuated five years, the second ten years, and the
third fifteen years after the signature of the treaty. Lloyd George
was dismayed to find Wilson agreeing in his absence to such an
extended commitment, but all his efforts in June to modify the
arrangement were of no avail.

Equally vigorous controversy was aroused by the disarmament clauses of the treaty, which were introduced by the words:
"In order to render possible the initiation of a general limitation
of armaments of all nations, Germany undertakes strictly to
observe the military, naval and air Clauses which follow."[1]

---

[1] The cautious statement of general aims quoted above was amplified by the
Allied Reply to the German Observations on 16 June: "The Allied and Associated
Powers wish to make it clear that their requirements in regard to German armaments were not made solely with the object of rendering it impossible for Germany
to resume her policy of military aggression. They are also the first steps towards
that general reduction and limitation of armaments which they seek to bring about
as one of the most fruitful preventives of war, and which it will be one of the first
duties of the League of Nations to promote." *The Treaty of Peace Between the Allied
and Associated Powers and Germany*, p. 268. H.M.S.O., 1920.

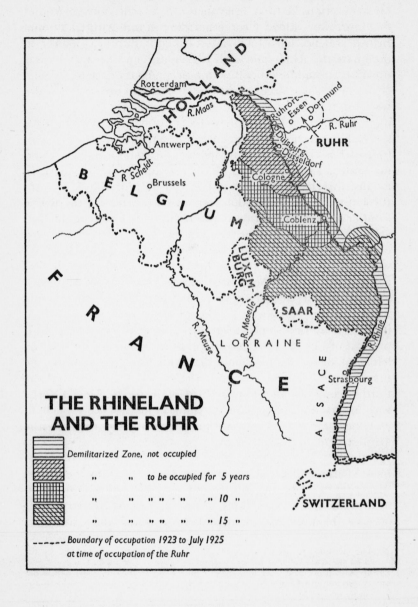

THE RHINELAND
AND THE RUHR

	Demilitarized Zone, not occupied
	,, ,, to be occupied for 5 years
	,, ,, ,, ,, ,, 10 ,,
	,, ,, ,, ,, ,, 15 ,,

------ Boundary of occupation 1923 to July 1925
at time of occupation of the Ruhr

Argument centred on the question of control of German armaments (France wished for a permanent control, which Wilson rejected on grounds of justice and Lloyd George on grounds of practicability), and on the type of German army that should be permitted. Marshal Foch considered that the German army should be a short-service army recruited by conscription to a maximum of two hundred thousand men: this would produce a non-professional force, and was the only democratic method of raising an army and spreading its burdens. Lloyd George and Wilson both advocated a long-service army to a maximum of one hundred thousand recruited by voluntary enlistment: in their view the abolition of conscription would reduce German militarism, and thus make a renewal of aggression less likely. (It is, of course, natural that French and British views about land forces should be thus opposed: the French need and tradition, especially since Carnot's *levée en masse* in 1793, has been for large land forces for metropolitan defence, whereas the British have required not a large standing army at home, being defended by the Channel, but a small highly trained army for easy transport and effective action in any part of the world.) The weight of Anglo-American agreement naturally carried the day, and a compromise was reached on the question of control by requiring Germany to accept any investigation that the Council of the League might deem necessary. These provisions, running counter to deeply felt French opinions, did not increase such sense of security as she derived from the treaty.

This security was now to be disrupted at its foundations. We have seen how France abandoned her demand for the Rhine frontier only in exchange for an Anglo-American guarantee against German aggression, a good exchange in the mind of Clemenceau, whose prime object was to retain the support of Britain and the United States. (None the less the provisions in the treaty to which the great French war leader had persuaded Britain and the United States to agree were deemed so inadequate by French political opinion that he was defeated in the Chamber in January 1920 and forced to resign.) The United States guarantee was, of course, annulled with the Senate's rejection of the Versailles treaty in November 1919 and again in March 1920. The British guarantee was contingent on that of the United States, and with the cancellation of the latter

Lloyd George took the legally justified course of withdrawing the British guarantee also (a striking example of the over-mastering concern of Britain with her overseas commitments and with the attitude of the United States, as compared with her interests in Europe). France was thus left with no assurance of support from Britain or the United States against any re-newed German threat, and with no defence against Germany's superior military potential beyond the temporary occupation of the left bank and the demilitarization of that area and the fifty-kilometre strip on the right bank. In these circumstances she was unwilling to relax any other terms of the treaty, of which the reparations clauses were one, or to embark on any significant measure of disarmament that would further reduce her defences against German power. Moreover, the unco-opera-tive attitude of the German government to the Allied Disarma-ment Commissions, the success with which the German General Staff preserved its tradition and existence under various camou-flages, the rise of para-military formations in Germany, and, after the treaty of Rapallo in April 1922, the secret but generally suspected military training and experimentation, and construction of forbidden armaments, by Germans on Russian soil—none of these was likely to encourage French confidence in German good faith. But in Britain the economic attractions of disarmament became steadily more apparent, and public opinion led by the Labour party was demanding progress. At length, recognizing that little advance could be made without some satisfaction of France's security requirements, Lloyd George in December 1921 offered France an unconditional guarantee against direct German aggression, without United States support.

The negotiations for an Anglo-French pact which this offer initiated laid down the lines of British policy towards Europe which were followed until March 1939, and epitomized the differences between the British and French points of view. Briand's reply to the offer made four main points. In the first place, the guarantee should be bilateral: this reflected the injury to French pride thought to be done by the form of the Anglo-American offer of 1919, and caused no particular conflict be-tween the two countries, though Britain was not greatly inter-ested. Secondly, the guarantee was to apply against indirect aggression also, by which Briand meant that an attack on France's close ally in the east, Poland, should be considered an attack on herself. Thirdly, any contravention of the Versailles treaty was to be equivalent to direct aggression. Finally, the alliance should be complemented by a General Staff *entente*. Britain's reply crystallized the issues. In no circumstances would Britain guarantee the unstable east, partly because her world interests were too wide to permit her to undertake large European commitments, and partly because she did not wish to encourage the division of Europe into two *blocs*; she would not, secondly, undertake to act in automatic defence of the Versailles *status quo*, and particularly of the demilitarized zone—the impression was growing in Britain that Versailles was by no means perfect; thirdly, she would not enter into General Staff conversations, primarily because they would be likely to give France the initiative in invoking a *casus fœderis*. To France, however, no guarantee was of value without a military convention because only then was immediate assistance ensured, and only immediate assistance could prevent a swift German initial success and a renewed occupation of the north-eastern industrial regions. The negotiations accordingly broke down, and it is of the greatest significance that no Anglo-French alliance existed in the whole inter-war period, a potent factor in France's apparent intransigence in the 'twenties, and dependence on British policies in the 'thirties. Britain did participate in the international guarantee system of Locarno, but in effect she abandoned even that in 1936. In that year a military alliance was tentatively formulated, but it met strong popular and political opposition in Great Britain, and such contacts as were made remained with no more binding political cover than an exchange of assurances. On the part of Britain the negotiations revealed the concern she felt for her world-wide commitments (supported now by reduced resources), the deference she necessarily paid to the views of the Dominions, the increasing impatience with French policy towards Germany and the beginnings of doubt about the Versailles treaty and of sympathy with the German point of view, and finally the outright refusal to undertake any commitments in Europe east of the Rhine. Each of these views persisted until the months immediately preceding the Second World War; they derived from the tradition of British policies as affected by her post-1918 situation and interpreted by unimaginative statesmen; in the 'twenties they seemed not unreasonable, but in the changed circumstances of the 'thirties they were to prove wholly disastrous.

In the meantime, discussions under the auspices of the League of Nations had clearly shown the unwillingness of France to enter any important disarmament agreement while her security requirements remained wholly unsatisfied. In September 1923 the most notable British supporter of the League of Nations, Lord Robert Cecil (now Viscount Cecil of Chelwood), accordingly joined with the French Colonel Réquin in preparing the Draft Treaty of Mutual Assistance. This treaty, designed to strengthen and speed up the working of the security provisions of the Covenant, attempted a definition of aggression, proposed a joint and several undertaking by the signatories to assist the object of an attack, and bound the League Council to act within four days of any notification of aggression. The object of the draft treaty was to permit states to disarm in proportion to the degree of security offered: the *status quo* powers, France, Belgium and Czechoslovakia, gave it their support; Italy and Japan accepted with reservations; Germany said that the treaty was irrelevant in her case, since she had no armaments (an assertion that was not true even in 1923); but the reaction of the United Kingdom and the Dominions was decisive.

As early as 1921, the nations of the Commonwealth had supported a Scandinavian-sponsored resolution under which, although sanctions against an aggressor remained automatically applicable, the Council should decide on the manner in which sanctions should be put into effect. The support given to this interpretative resolution by the United Kingdom and the Dominions demonstrated their concern lest, as a world association with world-wide interests, they might find their limited resources concentrated on a local and seemingly unimportant issue, thus exposing themselves to greater dangers nearer home; moreover, the absence of the United States meant that economic sanctions might be of little value unless the hazard of interference with United States trade were undertaken, and that the major burdens of League action must fall on the only other world naval power, the United Kingdom. The members of the Commonwealth therefore felt at this time that they must retain within their own hands the decision whether their military forces should be employed in a dispute or not. There was little prospect then that they would accept so loose and wide an extension of commitments as that involved by the draft treaty, and their rejection was naturally decisive.

It was a Labour government that rejected the draft treaty, but nevertheless Labour's advent to power altered the prospects. The chief Labour aspiration in the field of international affairs since 1919 had been the promotion of disarmament (reflecting the strong pacifist element within the British Labour movement), and the party had come to realize the need for meeting some of the French security requirements if the cause of disarmament were to be advanced. Using some of the ideas of the draft treaty, the new British Prime Minister and Foreign Secretary, Ramsay MacDonald, with the practical assistance of his Home Secretary, Arthur Henderson, prepared with M. Edouard Herriot (head of the *Cartel des Gauches* which had recently come to power in France) the outlines of a new plan, later known as the Geneva Protocol. The Protocol, brilliantly drafted by the Greek and Czech delegates at Geneva, Politis and Benesh, rested upon the trilogy of arbitration, security and disarmament. Compulsory arbitration was to be made the test of aggression: the signatories were jointly and severally to undertake to assist any disputant who was willing to submit the dispute to independent arbitration but was nevertheless attacked. This automatic and immediate decision on aggression would afford a good measure of security and would make disarmament possible.

The chances for acceptance of the Protocol seemed good. Britain had been partly responsible for initiating the project, and even the ex-enemy states were not hostile despite the consequent stabilization of existing frontiers (for arbitration was not to be applicable in questions of treaty revision): thus Count Apponyi, for Hungary, later declared that the rule of law was preferable to a state of anarchy even if frontier stabilization ensued, for regulation in an atmosphere of peace would still be possible.[1] The League Assembly accepted the Protocol on 2 October 1924, and Briand for France was the first to affix his initials.

At the general election on 4 November, however, the British

---

[1] See Toynbee, A. J. (ed.), *Survey of International Affairs, 1924*, p. 61. O.U.P., 1926.

Labour government was defeated, and the new Conservative Foreign Secretary, Austen Chamberlain, asked for time to consider the implications of the Protocol. This consideration, and the reaction of the Dominions to the project, led to the Conservative rejection on 12 March 1925. The Dominions' response was nowhere favourable. Canada disliked the rigidity of the Protocol's provisions for economic and military sanctions, particularly in view of the absence from the League of the United States. South Africa objected to the impairment of sovereignty implied by the Protocol, considered that nations at present outside the League would be less likely to join, and flatly refused any participation in international obligations entailing intervention by the Union in matters that only remotely concerned her. Australia was unwilling to undertake greater obligations than those of the Covenant so long as some great powers were not members of the League, and deprecated any proposals that would tend to make the League less of a moral agency and more of an organization for the imposition of pains and penalties. New Zealand refused to accept the compulsory jurisdiction of the Permanent Court at the Hague lest it should contest the validity of New Zealand's immigration laws and of Britain's traditional position on belligerent rights at sea.[1] It is often argued that, had the Labour government not been defeated, the Protocol would have been ratified by Britain and thereafter by the League, with immeasurable consequences for the history of the world: it is possible that this ratification might have taken place, but even had the Labour government remained in power, the attitude of the Dominions must necessarily have received the weightiest consideration.

Be that as it may, the Protocol was in fact rejected, and became just another abandoned security project. Chamberlain's speech of rejection, however, was not barren of constructive ideas, and clearly showed the direction of the new British government's thinking. "Since the general provisions of the Covenant cannot be stiffened with advantage, and since the 'extreme cases' with which the League may have to deal will probably affect certain nations or groups of nations more nearly than others, His Majesty's Government conclude that the best

[1] Comd. 2458, 1925. *Protocol for the Pacific Settlement of International Disputes. Correspondence relating to the position of the Dominions.*

way of dealing with the situation is, with the co-operation of the League, to supplement the Covenant by making special arrangements in order to meet special needs. . . . And, in the opinion of His Majesty's Government, these objects can best be attained by knitting together the nations most immediately concerned, and whose differences might lead to a renewal of strife, by means of treaties framed with the sole object of maintaining, as between themselves, an unbroken peace."[1] No clearer statement could be found of the British preference for limited, regional security arrangements, as opposed to blanket, world-wide commitments. After a brief delay, this speech of Chamberlain's was followed up by a proposal from Stresemann for a multilateral regional guarantee on the lines of Chamberlain's suggestion. In the negotiations that followed Stresemann's initiative, Britain refused a renewed attempt by Briand to obtain a British guarantee for eastern Europe, and France showed herself willing to accept a stabilization limited to the west—running counter to all her previously expressed opinions—only if Germany became a member of the League. This Germany was hesitant to do, partly because of the state of her armaments, but more because of her relations with the U.S.S.R.; but eventually she agreed to enter the League on an interpretation of Article 16, the sanctions article, stating that each state member of the League was bound to support Covenant action "loyally and effectively . . . to an extent which is compatible with its military situation and which takes its geographical position into account."[2] The complex of agreements known as the Locarno treaties was accordingly initialled on 16 October 1925 and signed on 1 December. They comprised a Western Pact of Mutual Guarantee under which the Franco-German frontier and the demilitarized zone of the Rhineland were declared permanent and inviolable and were guaranteed by Britain and Italy; a Draft Collective Note from the powers embodying the Article 16 interpretation; Arbitration Conventions between Germany on the one hand and France, Belgium, Poland and Czechoslovakia on the other; and Franco-Polish and Franco-Czech Treaties of Mutual Guarantee in the case of failure of the foregoing agreements.[3]

[1] League of Nations *Official Journal*, 6th Yr. No. 4: xxxiii, Cl., p. 450.
[2] *League of Nations Treaty Series*, Vol. 54, p. 301.
[3] For full details of the Locarno agreements see *League of Nations Treaty Series*, Vol. 54, pp. 289-363.

The Final Protocol included the words: "The representatives of the Governments represented here declare their firm conviction that the entry into force of these treaties and conventions will . . . hasten on effectively the disarmament provided for in Article 8 of the Covenant of the League of Nations. They undertake to give their sincere co-operation to the work relating to disarmament already undertaken by the League of Nations and to seek the realisation thereof in a general agreement."[1] A Preparatory Commission for a World Disarmament Conference was accordingly established on 12 December 1925.

Thus by the end of 1925 British policies were apparently achieving great successes. The temporary Dawes settlement of the reparations problem[2] had set on foot a startlingly rapid economic recovery in Germany and ushered in a quinquennium of economic expansion all over the world. In the resulting easing of political disputes, and with the aid of more conciliatory governments in Germany and France, Britain had been able to achieve in the Locarno treaties an amelioration of political disputes without herself undertaking any commitment beyond the Rhine. The way was thereby opened to world disarmament, the project to which, for economic and pacifist reasons, the British people was most closely wedded. The basic object of British policy, which at this time seemed within sight of achievement, was the establishment of lasting peace through the consent of all nations in a just international system.[3] In pursuit of this policy Britain consistently showed her unwillingness to keep Germany in lasting subjection: such an attempt was economically undesirable, since it would create a centre of economic depression in Europe; it was militarily unnecessary, the German fleet having been destroyed, and Britain being protected by the Channel; it was psychologically distasteful and unwise, the British dislike of lasting ill-will being stimulated by books such as that of Keynes[4] and encouraged by statesmen fearing the advance of Communism in a harshly treated Germany;

[1] *League of Nations Treaty Series*, Vol. 54, p. 299.
[2] See Chapter 3, pp. 41-43.
[3] A penetrating and scholarly analysis of British, French and German relations is to be found in Jordan, W. M., *Great Britain, France and the German Problem*, O.U.P., 1943, on which this and the succeeding chapter have heavily drawn.
[4] See Chapter 3, p. 35 n.

finally, it would prevent the re-emergence of any balance of power in Europe and would perpetuate the hegemony of France. The need to satisfy the legitimate claims of all nations, especially Germany, was made more urgent by the weakness of collective security without the support of the United States; and with the consequent heavy burden that would be imposed on the British fleet should action be required, Britain refused to accept any binding commitments in Europe beyond the Rhine. The League of Nations, lastly, was viewed primarily as an agency for peaceful change, not for preserving the *status quo*. In all these policies Britain received essential support from the Dominions, who were isolated from Europe and faced different problems; but it should be noted that the British policy inevitably led back to a German ascendancy in Europe, a conclusion which France clearly recognized.

The almost universal welcome with which the Locarno treaties were greeted concealed the new and old international disputes persisting beneath the surface. A discordant note was immediately struck by Poland's resistance to Germany's admission to the League Council as a permanent member if she did not herself acquire similar status. The stabilization of Germany's western frontier under British and Italian guarantee with no equivalent stabilization in the east (the application of arbitration to matters of treaty revision was not now excluded, as in the Geneva Protocol, and Germany had only promised not to alter her eastern frontier by force) aroused Polish fears that German eyes might be turned eastwards; while the very improvement in Franco-German relations, and the prospect of developing Franco-German collaboration in the Council, weakened the foundations of the Franco-Polish Alliance, so long as Polish-German relations remained bad. The wrangle was ended in September 1926 only by making Poland and Spain eligible for immediate re-election to the Council and thus giving them semi-permanent status. In the same month Briand had a wide-ranging discussion with Stresemann at Thoiry covering the Saar, the Rhineland and reparations, but the conversation achieved little but disillusionment, partly owing to popular opposition in France to a policy of concessions. The rivalry between France and Italy in North Africa and in the Balkans persisted. These various developments all contributed to the dissipation of the complete international confidence necessary to any effective disarmament—which would reduce the ability of each individual state to defend itself—and consequently little progress was made in the Preparatory Commission for the Disarmament Conference.

Discussion in the Preparatory Commission centred on three issues, all of them alread familiar. The question of how to define effectives in an army paralleled the Versailles dispute over a long- or short-service army for Germany: France maintained that effectives should be defined as those men actually serving in the army at any one time, Britain and the United States that all men with military training should be included in the definition. So long as Britain and the United States (and for that matter Germany) had long-service, volunteer armies, and France a short-service, conscript army with large reserves, little accommodation on this issue seemed probable. A second repeated Versailles controversy was that of control of disarmament: France insisted that no disarmament could be considered without the institution of effective methods of supervision, but the United States was unwilling to participate in any control scheme, and Italy refused to accept any control over her own armaments. Dispute, thirdly, persisted over the method of naval limitation, Britain (with her need for a given minimum number of cruisers) insisting that limitation should be by classes of vessels, whereas France maintained that limitation should be by total tonnages. No reconciliation of these three opposed views had been found when the U.S.S.R. and Germany joined the Commission in November 1927 and March 1928 respectively. Litvinov for the U.S.S.R. immediately introduced a new note into the discussion by proposing, for propaganda purposes,[1] the complete all-round abolition of armaments by land, sea and in the air. Germany supported the proposals, hoping to force the Allies either into genuine disarmament, or into legalizing rearmament for herself. The German and Soviet pressure, and their open collusion, forced Paul-Boncour for France into the

[1] This purpose was explicitly recognized at the sixth Congress of the Comintern in 1928: ". . . It goes without saying that not a single communist thought that the imperialists would accept the Soviet disarmament plan. . . . [The second proposal for partial disarmament] was not a concession to pacifism; on the contrary, it served to expose in particular the attitude of the great powers to small and oppressed nations." *Kommunisticheski International v. dokumentakh, 1919–32,* pp. 825–6, Moscow, 1933.

open to say that major disarmament was only possible with the degree of security afforded by the Geneva Protocol, but in July Britain and France reached a compromise by which Britain accepted the French definition of effectives and France agreed to the British proposals for naval limitation. This agreement brought no advance, because the United States and Germany objected to one half, and the United States and Italy objected to the other. Little progress was made during 1929, while the negotiations on naval disarmament which led to the London treaty were proceeding between Britain and the United States,[1] and although a great mass of technical material had been handled no agreement had been reached even on the principles, let alone on scales, of disarmament before the World Economic Crisis broke in 1929.

The World Disarmament Conference met on 2 February 1932 in conditions far less favourable than during the period of controversy in the Preparatory Commission before 1930. The World Economic Crisis had consequences political, social and psychological that far outran the economic limits within which the crisis had been born. Moreover, the influence of Britain and the United States over French policy was lessened, since France retained her financial strength into 1932. The fears that had inspired French policy since 1919 were by now powerfully reinforced. Germany had made great economic strides since 1924, and was now openly rearming while professing not to be;[2] internal unrest was increasing in Germany, and the Nationalists and the Nazis were becoming steadily more powerful; the danger of Soviet-German friendship had been reaffirmed in the disarmament discussions; Italy was becoming increasingly bellicose, not merely in the bombastic words of Mussolini about the beauty of cannon but in the laying down of new naval tonnages; the security conferred by the occupation of the Rhineland had

---

[1] See Chapter 6, pp. 78-79.

[2] At the end of 1931 the British Military Attaché in Berlin gave as one example of evasion of the military clauses of Versailles the issuing to all units in 1931 of a new anti-tank gun complete with laying gear, sights, carriage and shield, but with wooden barrels and trails. The genuine barrels and trails being secretly issued and kept in regimental stores, within a few hours every unit could be equipped with an effective anti-tank weapon upon which all training except firing had been completed. Woodward, E. L. and Butler, R., *Documents on British Foreign Policy, 1919-1939*, Second Series, Vol. II, Appx. 4, p. 517.

ended with the evacuation of the third zone on 30 June 1930, five years early, as part of the Young settlement of reparations. But not least significant both of French fears and of the grounds for them was Briand's proposal for European union in 1930, and the reactions to it. His main suggestion was for the establishment of a federal governmental organ, the powers of which should be primarily economic, but only within the bounds of political requirements. The *status quo* powers, Poland and the Little Entente, strongly favoured the proposal. The countries with extra-European ties—Spain, Portugal, the Netherlands, Britain—replied cautiously, stressing the primacy of economic over political issues, London adding the opinion that the proposed functions of the union added little to those already performed by the League. The revisionist and ex-enemy countries —Italy, Germany, Hungary, Austria, Bulgaria—replied that there could be no stabilization of present frontiers, and that the Soviet Union and Turkey should be included. Whatever Briand's intentions in fact were, the various replies showed that the revisionist countries feared, and the *status quo* countries believed, that the result of such a union would be to confirm French hegemony, the restriction to members of the League being particularly ominous since it excluded Germany's friend, the U.S.S.R., and Italy's friend, Turkey. This French attempt at security in a different form was referred to a League commission and there quietly expired.

In these greatly worsened conditions it was hardly to be expected that French policy would now offer concessions to disarmament that she had not hitherto felt able to make without some greater satisfaction of her security requirements than the partial one of Locarno. The weakness of collective security had been sharply pointed by the Japanese defiance of the League in Manchuria: as a peculiarly inauspicious omen their bombardment of Shanghai caused the first session of the Disarmament Conference to be postponed for two hours in order that the League Council could meet. But not only had French policy hardened behind the need for security first, but Germany under the pressure of political and economic crisis at home was now pressing for an immediate recognition of her equality of status with the other powers. In order to enforce this demand, the Papen government withdrew its delegates from the Conference in July. In this atmosphere of tension and insecurity, France, through her Foreign Minister Paul-Boncour, made her last major effort to combine security with disarmament. The Paul-Boncour plan, presented in November, recognized the impracticability of uniform world-wide obligations, and proposed the creation of three sets of undertakings. The perimeter nations like the United States, who were exposed to few dangers, should only be required to break off relations with an aggressor; the more central nations, members of the League, should act according to the Covenant; the central group of precarious European countries should combine for mutual assistance and place forces at the disposal of the League. This security plan should be combined with a General Act of Arbitration and, in the field of disarmament, with short-service armies, destruction of mobile striking equipment, and permanent supervision with inspection.

The fundamentals of British policy, however, like those of France and Germany, had only been confirmed by the World Economic Crisis and developments since 1929. The British reaction to the Briand proposal for European union had shown the unchanged assumptions of Britain's thinking about Europe: the direct influence of Germany's financial crisis in the spring and summer of 1931 on the British crash in the early autumn had powerfully reinforced Britain's concern for economic health in Germany. Britain remained a firm believer in disarmament, for the same economic and pacifist reasons as in the previous decade, but the British government recognized that German co-operation could only be obtained through accepting the principle of equality, and that disarmament without German co-operation was impossible. A formula was found in December for bringing Germany back to the Conference by defining one of its aims as being the achievement of "equality of rights in a system which would provide security for all nations", and Britain thus achieved a temporary success in her prime aim of reconciling Germany with her former enemies.

But the British success was short-lived. This major victory for Schleicher's government in Germany—the recognition of equality—did not save him from the intrigue that brought Hitler to the Chancellery on 30 January 1933. The British response to the Paul-Boncour plan, in the second place, rejecting the concept of world collective security and placing renewed emphasis on regionalism, was taken by the French as sabotage of collective security only equalled by the previous British rejection of the Geneva Protocol. The prospects for a favourable French approach to disarmament thus gravely worsened with the reaffirmation of the British view, and the advent to power of the Hitler régime—whose character and aims the French fully understood, if they did not anticipate the degree to which Hitler would command the allegiance of the German people with his adept mixture of terror, lying and achievement. In an attempt to stop the rot, MacDonald himself went to Geneva in March 1933 and gave his name to a hurriedly produced plan which he outlined on the 16th. The MacDonald plan for the first time included figures as well as principles. Qualitative limits were suggested for various types of weapons; naval limits were proposed; all states were to have short-service armies, the French and German being each two hundred thousand men; there should be no increase of armaments during discussion of qualitative limitations. France accepted the plan as a basis for discussion, but would not destroy any heavy material until a supervisory system had been tested and while her militia reduction was being effected, would agree to no German increase in the meantime, and would not in any case decrease her armaments while Germany persisted in her illegal rearmament. These reservations meant a postponement of German equality to an unknown date, but the early measures of the Nazis, in contrast with their pacific professions, gave force to the French view. Italy, the United States and Britain accordingly agreed that the draft convention should be valid over two periods, and that the former Allies should reduce their armaments only after experience of the supervisory system. On 14 October the British Foreign Secretary, Sir John Simon, therefore proposed that Germany should have a short-service conscript army of two hundred thousand men, that all countries should agree to supervision, that there should be no Allied reductions until the supervisory system had been tested, but that Germany should eventually have full equality with all other powers. On this same day Hitler withdrew his representatives both from the Disarmament Conference and from the League, and his decision received an overwhelming endorsement in a referendum in which the majority of voters probably genuinely approved his action.

The second German withdrawal in effect killed the Disarmament Conference, although its President, the former Labour Foreign Secretary, Arthur Henderson, kept the issue alive through visiting the capitals of Europe during the winter months. The German budget of March 1934, however, published figures of large appropriations for armaments, and on 17 April France reacted in a declaration by her Foreign Minister, Louis Barthou, that France could accept no legalization of German rearmament and would henceforth seek security through her own methods. This declaration was apparently necessitated by domestic considerations, but the British government professed to believe that the door at least to limitation of armament had not been closed until Barthou slammed it shut.[1] Irritation with Paris caused a revival of sympathy for Berlin, and on 3 February 1935 Britain induced France to move further down the road and agree to a joint communiqué proposing, with security guarantees, an air pact (thus to some extent implicitly recognizing Germany's right to an air force), and waiving the demand for an interim period before Allied disarmament should start. The effect of this communiqué was, however, nullified by a British white paper on defence on 4 March, naming Germany as a military danger, and by a debate in the French Chamber of Deputies on doubling the length of military service to prevent the loss of effectives caused by the *classes creuses* (the small classes born in 1915 onwards). On 9 March the Nazis first openly violated a treaty by announcing the existence of a German air force, and on 16 March they issued a decree re-introducing conscription.[2]

British governments from 1920 to 1934 were all advocates of disarmament, though with some variations in emphasis and approach. But just as the United States could afford, in her greater geographical security, to press Britain further along the road to naval disarmament than the island Kingdom was willing to go,[3] so Britain, in her greater immunity from European

[1] Barthou apparently was willing to explore with Britain the possibilities of limitation of armament as distinct from disarmament, but the Prime Minister, Doumergue, insisted on the 17 April declaration. Barthou yielded, not daring to disrupt the government of National Unity that had been formed to combat the effects of the Stavisky scandal in February. See François-Poncet, A., *Souvenirs d'une Ambassade à Berlin*, pp. 175-8. Flammarion, Paris, 1946.

[2] See Chapter 8, pp. 100-1.

[3] See Chapter 6, *passim*.

attack, showed far less heed than France for the risks and dangers of restoring German power. The governments of Mac-Donald seemed to appreciate more fully than those of Baldwin the fact that the cause of disarmament could not obtain the adherence of France without some strengthening of collective security, but it remains an open question whether even a majority Labour government could have afforded to accept such an instrument as the Protocol in the face of Dominion opposition. Without some such security undertaking, the British desire for disarmament was bound to meet persistent French opposition; growing irritation with France, combined with the pressure of economic circumstances, steadily increased British sympathy with Germany and pressed British policy towards Berlin and away from Paris. The ultimate cause of the disaster of 1939 was that the World Economic Crisis produced conditions that encouraged this trend while simultaneously facilitating the accession to power of a megalomaniac dictator in Germany to co-operate with whom meant suicide.

The different approaches to the problem of disarmament represented the different defence needs of the various countries. France, as the power facing the most dangerous potential threat on land, naturally appeared as the intransigent party in the field of land armaments, but Britain and even the United States held as tenaciously to their own points of view in the naval spheres, which were to them more vital. The ultimate lesson of the negotiations was that, so long as the world remained divided into independent sovereign states, governments would insist on maintaining a certain level of armament to which they would arm and below which they would not disarm. Even had governments been willing to compromise the safety of their countries as they and their experts understood it (and it may be questioned whether any independent national government may properly take such action), their peoples were not, whether they lived in the United States, in Britain, in France or in Germany. Advance would be possible only within the framework of an effective world security system, willingly accepted by all great powers, whether such a system did or did not entail some merging of sovereignties.

Chapter 3

REPARATIONS

THE DIFFERENCE of weight accorded by Britain and France respectively to economic and political issues was even more strikingly evident in the question of reparations from Germany than in the twin problem of security and disarmament. Many Frenchmen believed that the unequal balance of economic strength between their own country and Germany could to some extent be reduced by the transfer of German wealth to France through reparation payments and by deliveries of goods in compensation for destroyed productive capacity. Thus even the question of reparations had some small political content. An unresolved inconsistency of policy, however, underlay the French attitude. Her demands for heavy reparations could be met only by a great expansion in Germany's productive capacity, such as occurred between 1924 and 1929. Such an expansion would not cause France any very great fears from the point of view of German commercial competition, for she was not a world trader on the scale either of Britain or of Germany; but it would evidently entail in the long run an increase in that very disparity in economic strength which France so greatly feared. Of the political implications of German stabilization and recovery Frenchmen were well aware; of the economic inconsistency between the demand for heavy reparations and the fear of German economic power most seem to have been ignorant.

British policy showed itself to be far more aware of economic realities than that of France.[1] After a brief period of folly immediately after Lloyd George's coupon election at the end of 1918, British governments consistently pressed for a moderate

---

[1] The economic insight and political myopia of the British on the one hand, and the economic blindness and political clarity of view of the French on the other, are perhaps well illustrated by the contrast between J. M. Keynes's famous book *The Economic Consequence of the Peace*, Macmillan, 1919, and Etienne Mantoux's reply to it, *The Carthaginian Peace*, O.U.P., 1946.

and final settlement that would make possible Germany's economic recovery and thus forward the economic recovery of Europe and the world. Even in British policy, however, there existed an underlying conflict between the desire for reparations and for overcoming economic depression (for these German recovery was necessary), and the fear of the trade competition of a Germany restored to economic health. The exponents of the latter fear were, however, generally able to do little more than cause occasional delay or hesitancy in the major unfolding of policy in accordance with the first consideration. British and French policies were thus directly opposed over the objects and methods of reparations no less than over the desirability or necessity of guarantees of security against Germany, and over the timing and need for disarmament. The attitudes adopted by both countries to each of the three problems were constantly affected by developments in the other two.

The paying of indemnities in money and goods by the defeated party to the victor in war has been an accepted practice over the centuries. As in some previous settlements, the defeated party, Germany, was declared to be responsible for the war and was held consequentially liable for damage done during the war.[1] President Wilson's addresses on which the peace settlement was to be based had laid down the condition that Germany must restore Belgium, France, Serbia and Rumania, and that phrase had been clarified by the Allies in an interpretation agreed with President Wilson: "the President declared that the invaded territories must be restored as well as evacuated and freed, and the Allied Governments feel that no doubt ought to be allowed to exist as to what this provision implies. By it they understand that compensation will be made by Germany for all damage done to the civilian population of the Allies, and their property by the aggression of Germany by land, by sea, and from the air."[2] Under the principle of reparation of civilian damage, however, Great Britain's share would be a small one. To set against her colossal financial contribution she could claim only for her sunk and damaged merchant shipping, and

---

[1] It is not my concern here to argue the rights and wrongs of the war guilt clause. Most nations had some responsibility for the outbreak of war: among the nations the responsibility of some was very heavy, of others very light.

[2] Temperley, H. W. V. (ed.), *History of the Peace Conference of Paris*, Vol. I, p. 134. O.U.P., 1920.

for a small amount of bomb damage. Spurred by the promises he had made to the electorate, Lloyd George at first fought for the principle that Germany should be held accountable for the total cost of war-making, the proportion of that sum that Germany paid being subsequently divisible among the Allies according to their financial contributions to the war. The British Prime Minister was not unnaturally defeated in this proposal, but he then shifted his ground and successfully fought for the inclusion, within the framework of civilian damage, of the cost of pensions and separation allowances paid to wives and dependants of injured or killed ex-servicemen. The limits of German liability were thus broadly defined as compensation for devastation, destruction and damage to civilian property, compensation for merchant shipping sunk or damaged, and payment to an amount equal to the cost of pensions and separation allowances in the various Allied countries.

But agreement on the limits of Germany's liability was only the first step in the problem. There was no estimate in 1919 of the amount of this liability as defined, but it seemed highly probable that the amount would be considerably more than Germany could possibly manage to pay. Was Germany's liability then to be assessed according to the damage done, or according to her capacity to pay? If the latter, how could that be estimated? The French argued, with impeccable logic, that although Germany might not be able to pay in full the amounts for which she was liable, she should at least pay as much as she could towards it, and that it was impossible to say in 1919 how much she would be able to pay in later years. Therefore it was impossible in 1919 to fix the figure of Germany's total liability. Lloyd George at first on 29 March supported the French view, but by June he had joined the United States delegation in pressing for the fixing of a definite sum at once. It was indeed evident that if the amount for which Germany was to be liable was to vary according to the amount she was able to pay, then all incentive to efficiency, production and recovery would be destroyed, for the more she produced, the more she would have to pay. Lloyd George's change of front, however, in this as in other matters, came too late to affect the final settlement: after detailing various forms of reparations in kind (shipping, coal, reconstruction materials, cattle) the relevant clauses of the Versailles treaty laid down certain provisional figures for cash payments but with no upper limit, and remitted the whole problem to a special reparations commission whose task was to fix total amounts and methods of payment by 1 May 1921. The French view that the total liability could not be determined in 1919 thus prevailed, but some reflection of the United States and later British views appeared in the principles within which the Reparations Commission was to work—that they were to pay due regard to the economic life of Germany, that Germany had the right to present her case, and that reparations should not last longer than one generation. The United States delegation dared not press their opposition to the French view lest by so doing they should have opened the whole question of inter-allied indebtedness, which they had hitherto successfully excluded from discussion in the reparations context.[1]

By 5 May 1921, when the London schedule of payments was presented, British policy after this initial uncertainty had moved on to the lines which it followed until the reparations question was closed in July 1932. At the end of 1920 Wilson had, under domestic pressure, coldly rebuffed Lloyd George's attempt to have Britain's war debt obligations scaled down, and Britain henceforth felt herself unable to remit any of the interest payments due to herself without corresponding remission from the United States; but within those limits she desired sweeping reductions in both reparations and war debts. Above all, Lloyd George insisted that only a permanent settlement of the problem could restore Germany's credit. But the London schedule of payments in effect still left the total liability undetermined: the figure named was £6,600 million, but clearly Germany could not pay such a sum, and the commission proposed that Germany should be immediately liable to make payments on only rather more than one-third of the nominal figure. In effect, therefore, the amount Germany would have to pay was still unknown, the last remnants of confidence, internal and external, in the German economy were dissipated, and with the first cash payment duly made on 31 August 1921 the fall in value of the German mark began.

---

[1] Baruch, Bernard M., *The Making of the Reparation and Economic Sections of the Treaty*, p. 71. Harper, N.Y., 1920.

The conflict between British and French policy grew steadily more acute. France maintained that the German government and German industrialists were deliberately undermining the German economy in order to make reparations payments impossible and thus force a cancellation of the whole obligation; Britain considered that neither economic recovery nor reparations could be expected from Germany so long as investors had no confidence, and there could be no confidence in an economy whose production was indefinitely mortgaged for unlimited amounts. The French need for reparations was made more acute by the large reconstruction schemes that the government had launched in anticipation of reparations receipts; the British desire for European economic recovery was spurred by the mounting figures of British unemployed in 1921 with their serious social and political consequences. Britain therefore considered reasonable the repeated German requests for moratoria in the latter part of 1921, but France remained unwilling to believe in their necessity. Briand was, however, induced to discuss a moratorium at the Cannes conference between 6 and 13 January 1922, but rumours of the discussions caused such a storm in France that Briand was forced to return in the middle of the conference, and in Paris he met a hostile vote in the Chamber of Deputies and was replaced as Prime Minister by Poincaré on 11 January.

The sharpness of the French reaction to Briand's attempt at conciliation revealed that British and French political and public opinions were divided in their attitudes towards Germany no less than their governments. The task of reconciling the opposed policies was thus made all the harder. Nevertheless the British government made two attempts in the course of 1922 to break the deadlock. The first of these, the Genoa conference from 10 April to 19 May, was doomed to failure from the start. In launching this conference (his last major political initiative) Lloyd George had four main objects in view: first, to settle the reparations controversy; secondly, to promote economic recovery by establishing economic and political relations with the U.S.S.R.; thirdly, to revise the peace treaties where necessary in the interests of economic recovery; fourthly, to divert attention from the collapse of his policy in Asia Minor. The first and third items were excluded from the agenda on the insistence of Poincaré, and negotiations on the second broke down for reasons that will be discussed in a later chapter.[1]

Lloyd George's last attempt at a wide-ranging economic settlement thus failed ignominiously, but one further effort was made in the lifetime of his government to break the reparations deadlock. On 1 August 1922, in the so-called Balfour note, Great Britain announced to the interested powers that she would be satisfied to receive in reparations and interest on war debts owing to her only so much as she was herself required to pay in interest on her own war debts to the United States. This was a remarkably generous offer, for Britain was proposing to renounce at one stroke some three-quarters of the total amounts due to her; but to France and the other Allies the matter bore a different aspect. From their point of view, the more Germany paid in reparations, the less they would have to pay in debt interest to Great Britain; the less Germany paid, the more France and the others must pay to make up the fixed total. The effect of the Balfour note was therefore still further to harden Poincaré's determination to make Germany meet her obligations. On 14 November Germany appealed for a four years' postponement of payments, and for a final fixing of her total liability which, she said, was necessary to restore German credit and confidence in the mark. At a conference in London between 8 and 11 December British and French views remained opposed, and finally a resolution of the reparations commission on 26 December declared Germany in default, the vote of the British representative, Sir John Bradbury, being cast against the resolution. This declaration of Germany's default was the justification for the Franco-Belgian occupation of the Ruhr, which began on 11 January 1923. Britain considered the occupation of the Ruhr illegal, since she remained unconvinced of the deliberate intention of the German government to default (which alone could justify forcible action), and her prophecy that the occupation would destroy Germany's capacity to pay any reparations at all proved wholly accurate. The occupation was met by passive resistance and a general strike financed by government printing of money, and the natural result was the final collapse of German credit and the German mark, which

[1] See Chapter 5, p. 62.

by 9 October was quoted at more than one billion to the dollar. Some stabilization was achieved in November with the issue of the Rentenmark, and the making of the Micum agreements— local settlements by industrial enterprises with the French authorities under which production slowly restarted—but the situation at the end of 1923 clearly demanded some fresh approach. Germany's mood of bitterness and despair found expression in the expansion of the Communist party, but still more in the rise of Hitlerism; Britain's need for European recovery was as imperative as ever; France recognized that the Poincaré policy of forcing Germany to meet her obligations had failed; even the United States was feeling some of the effects of Europe's poverty. All these factors led to the meeting of the Dawes committee in January 1924.

On 29 December 1922 the United States Secretary of State, Charles E. Hughes, had suggested in an address to the American Historical Association that there should be appointed a committee of eminent experts, not instructed by, and not binding, the governments of their countries, their purpose being to make recommendations about the reparations problem, recommendations that would carry weight because of the eminence of the committee and its deliberate mobilization of public opinion. This method was suggested primarily to avoid any commitment of the United States administration. The Dawes committee was established in accordance with the procedure suggested by Hughes, and thus United States representation was secured. Nowhere did the word "reparations" appear in the terms of reference of the committee, its tasks being to propose methods of balancing the German budget and restoring Germany's currency stability—but evidently any such proposal had to include an examination of the reparations problem.

In the work of the committee a prominent part was played by the leading British expert, Sir Josiah Stamp, but the plan proposed by the committee on 9 April 1924 did not confirm the repeatedly expressed opinion of the British and United States governments that only a permanent settlement of the reparations question could restore Germany's credit. The Dawes plan (which was accepted by MacDonald, Herriot and Stresemann on 9 August and came into operation on 31 October) fixed only the maximum that Germany could be required to pay in any one year, but did not fix (and had no need to within its terms of reference) the number of years for which Germany should pay, or the total sum. Confidence in the German economy was, however, restored by fixing a maximum annual liability, by making the question of transfer an Allied not a German responsibility,[1] and by raising an external loan for Germany of eight hundred million marks.

The Dawes plan worked smoothly until its supersession in May 1930, and the very smoothness of its working demonstrated the extent to which political issues had complicated the reparations problem since 1919. The French determination to make Germany pay according to the damage done (politically the only reasonable criterion) and not according to her capacity was proved impracticable; the British, United States and German insistence that only a permanent settlement and a known total obligation (an insistence inspired by different political motives in the case of each) could restore Germany's credit and make any reparations payments possible was proved incorrect. Only bitter experience forced the governments chiefly concerned to modify their extreme conditions and accept a compromise agreement. But it is important to see how in fact the Dawes plan did work. The actual transfer of wealth from Germany to the Allies on a major scale was possible only through the physical movement of capital goods (which was not favoured) or through a substantial export surplus. The latter was not achieved by Germany. But the transfer problem was none the less apparently solved, for Germany regularly made her due payments. She possessed the foreign exchange with which to make these payments only as a result of an enormous movement of foreign, mainly American, capital into Germany in the form of loans and investment: indeed, considerably more foreign capital flowed into Germany than reparations payments flowed out, the relative figures being 10.3 milliard Reichsmarks paid in reparations compared with an 18.2 milliard Reichsmark increase in Germany's foreign debt.[2] Thus while through the Dawes plan the German state reduced its foreign debt, it could

---

[1] Up to this time there had been persistent confusion in the phrase "what Germany could pay" between what could be raised by internal fiscal means and what could be transferred to Germany's creditors by export surpluses or in other ways.

[2] Woodward, E. L. and Butler, R., *Documents on British Foreign Policy, 1919-1939*, Second Series, Vol. II, Appx. II, p. 486.

do so only because German banks and through them commercial and industrial enterprises were increasing theirs. The effect of this heavy foreign investment was to produce a rapid reconstruction of German industry and enormous increases in prosperity, and thus to make possible Stresemann's fulfilment policy in comparative political stability (although the Nazis steadily increased their numbers throughout the period). On the other hand this reconstruction, and the heavy cartellization following upon the destruction of capital in 1923, provided the means by which the weapons of an aggressive expansionist policy could be furnished should such a policy be embraced by any future German government. With the apparent success of the Dawes plan Britain was well content, although the initiation of the plan owed little to British governmental action. Neither she nor the United States heeded the dangers of a revival of German power on a short-term hand-to-mouth basis (the vast bulk of the foreign capital flowing into Germany was loaned on short-term only) with no safeguards and with only limited conciliation of other matters in dispute: both welcomed the improvement in Franco-British and Franco-German relations which resulted from the temporary Dawes settlement of the reparations problem and which flowered into the western guarantee system of the Locarno treaties.

Successful though the interim Dawes scheme was, however, the need soon came to be felt for a permanent settlement of the problem. A combination of circumstances in 1928 and 1929 created the opportunity for a reopening of the question. The United States was becoming concerned at the amount of American capital flowing into Germany; France had just made a funding agreement with the United States by which she was to make payments on her war debts over a period of sixty-two years and, now knowing her debt liability, she wanted a permanent settlement of Germany's reparations liability extending over a similar period; Germany was willing to bargain a reparations settlement for an early evacuation of the occupied zones of the Rhineland; Britain maintained her favourable attitude to a permanent reparations settlement. These considerations led to the convening of the Young committee in 1929, Hjalmar Schacht being the German spokesman. After a threatened deadlock both over the amount and over various political conditions that Schacht tried to insert as the price of a settlement, agreement was reached on a total liability of £2,050 million to be paid over fifty-eight years, £660 million of this to be paid in annuities in all circumstances, the yearly amount varying according to the amounts due in war-debt payments to the United States. The report was signed on 7 June 1929, but the first governmental conference on the report at the Hague in August broke down because Snowden insisted on a higher percentage for Britain than was proposed. Agreement was, however, reached at the second Hague conference in January 1930, and on 9 May the Young plan came into force and superseded Dawes.

But this date was already six months after the crash on Wall Street which had launched the World Economic Crisis. The crash, even more than the great American boom of 1928, caused not merely a cessation of foreign lending but a calling-in of short-term loans to Washington. The resultant drain, together with other elements of the crisis, soon produced financial collapse in Vienna, and by the middle of 1931 a similar disaster was threatening Berlin. On the evening of 20 June President Hoover accordingly proposed from Washington a year's moratorium on all war debt and reparations payments. This proposal immediately received cordial and wholehearted approval from London. In Britain the sympathy for Germany and the dislike of the economic implications of both war debts and reparations had reached a point where many leading figures hoped for the cessation of both: in the words of Vansittart, Permanent Under-Secretary of State for Foreign Affairs: "I did not believe that . . . the present system [the Young plan] could endure for a couple of generations. Most observers had probably estimated that the present system would continue for some time only because no change of heart or attitude was to be expected on the part of the United States . . . that change of heart and attitude had come . . . with astonishing rapidity, and we could all only welcome it. . . ."[1] But France feared that once such a proposal as that of Hoover was accepted, German payments would never be resumed on the same scale, and that she might find herself in the future still saddled with war-debt obligations

[1] Woodward, E. L. and Butler, R., *Documents on British Foreign Policy, 1919-1939*, Second Series, Vol. II, p. 96.

when reparations payments had come to an end. Agreement to act on the moratorium proposal was thus provisionally reached only on 6 July, but by October, with the deepening of the crisis, even the French had come to accept the effective demise of the Young plan. In a visit to Washington in that month the French Premier Laval failed to induce Hoover to wipe the war debt slate clean, and the President's stand was endorsed by a vote in Congress on 22 December. Britain was, however, by now pressing for the complete abolition of all inter-governmental indebtedness arising from the war, and the accession to power of Herriot in France made more possible a settlement of reparations as the first step towards such an abolition.

A governmental conference accordingly met at Lausanne under the presidency of MacDonald, and despite political diffi-culties in both France and Germany, and notwithstanding the French fear of persisting war-debt obligations and the highly unhelpful attitude of von Papen, agreement was eventually reached on 9 July 1932, largely as a result of an intense effort of mediation by the British delegation between France and Germany. The agreement provided for the compounding of all Germany's reparations liabilities in a single payment of £150 million, but Herriot could only be persuaded to accept this virtual cancellation in return for an understanding with Britain, Italy and Belgium that ratification of the agreement was de-pendent on satisfactory arrangements being made between Germany's four chief creditor countries and their own creditors. The terms of this understanding, however, caused a storm in the United States, where they were viewed as blackmail, and any negotiation on war debts was impossible in this atmosphere of intense resentment and in an election year. The December 1932 debt instalments were paid by some countries, including Britain, but many others, including France and Belgium, de-faulted. In June and December 1933 Britain and Italy made token payments, saying that they were unable to pay in full but did not wish to prejudice agreement by defaulting, but in April 1934 the Johnson Act prohibited United States citizens from dealing in the foreign securities of defaulting countries. The attitude of which this Act was a symptom clearly showed the object of token payments to be unattainable, and all countries

45

except Finland accordingly defaulted in June 1934. Without any war-debt agreements the Lausanne agreement was never ratified, and since Hitler had come to power in January 1933, the £150 million was never paid.

War debts and reparations thus both ended in default and recrimination. After a brief period of irresponsibility immediately after the war British policy, with the support of British public opinion, had moved more swiftly towards economic sanity than that of any other country, but in face of French political and financial insecurity and the unyielding attitude of the United States, British diplomacy had been able to make little headway until the World Economic Crisis forced a solution. The reparations and war-debt questions were a major disruptive element in Anglo-French-American relations between 1919 and 1923, and again between 1929 and 1934, and the fate of the latter was perhaps the most important single cause of the extreme isolationism of the United States in the 'thirties, with all its disastrous consequences. Inter-governmental indebtedness was an important cause of the World Economic Crisis, which sowed the seeds for the Second World War, and the war guilt clause by which reparations were justified produced much German bitterness which was exploited by the Nationalists and by Hitler, and which intensified French fears of Germany. Such payments of reparations as were made by Germany contributed little to the real wealth of the recipients, being made possible only by loans to Germany; but these loans on the other hand made possible the recovery of Germany and the recreation of her war-making industrial capacity. Such payments of war debts as were made to the United States similarly contributed little to her prosperity, since her balance of trade remained favourable and they were therefore possible only on account of her own lending. These considerations were not fully appreciated by statesmen at the time, and still less by their peoples, but it was British policy that came closest to an understanding of basic economic realities, and at an earlier date.

Chapter 4

THE MIDDLE EAST

IN THEIR ATTITUDE towards the Middle East and the Arab world, as in their approaches to the German problem, Britain and France were fundamentally opposed. In both countries after the war twentieth-century ideas of colonial development for the benefit of the native populations as well as for the benefit of the administering power were taking root, but the differing colonial traditions of the two powers naturally led to different interpretations of the same principle. France believed that the white populations of Africa had a natural position of leadership, and that Africa's best hope of material and intellectual progress lay in wise guidance and education by European mentors. The object should be "to attain a harmonious symbiosis of the different races".[1] This conception was reinforced by the vital French concern for the security of the western Mediterranean, a security which could be adequately safeguarded only by the maintenance of a permanent position in North Africa. Any influences that might undermine that position, such as the encouragement of ignorant and short-sighted nationalism in other parts of the Arab world, must be uncompromisingly resisted.

The British conception of mutually beneficial Empire-building, on the other hand, recognizing both the appeal of nationalism and the weakness of the British Commonwealth in face of its world-wide problems, looked towards self-government for dependent peoples, British interests being safeguarded by close friendly relations under the aegis of treaties of alliance conferring economic and military privileges upon the former administering power. This policy of permitting, if not actively encouraging, local nationalism appeared to France a deliberately Machiavellian attempt by Great Britain to eject her from

[1] Montagne, R., "France, England and the Arab States" in *International Affairs*, July 1949, p. 287.

any position of influence in the Levant: it was to be resisted not merely because of the important French interests, cultural and economic, in Syria and the Lebanon,[1] but because of the serious repercussions in North Africa that the emergence of autonomous Arab states in the eastern Mediterranean might cause. Moreover, France retained some measure of her traditional interest in Egypt (from which she had been more or less unintentionally ousted by Britain in the 1880s), and Britain had now no desire to see French influence reappearing there or in the Suez Canal zone. Both countries, finally, were, as always, deeply interested in the régime that should govern the Straits. A deep-seated imperial rivalry (composed only in 1904 in the face of the common danger of Germany, which had now been removed) was thus in 1919 embittered by a fundamental conflict of methods and aims: "British principles," in the words of one authority, "while realist and self-interested, have in their working-out usually been ready to consider and be influenced by the salient needs and wishes of those [dependent] peoples. French colonial policy, on the other hand, has a certain idealist basis; but since that idealism is itself rooted in an excess of self-esteem, it is commonly not prepared to give consideration to conflicting claims and interests."[2]

The opposed views of France, however, were only the first of the difficulties with which British policy in the Middle East had to contend in the immediate post-war period. Three other powers were vitally interested in the disposition of the Asiatic and European provinces of the former Ottoman Empire. Of these one, the Soviet Union, was at first preoccupied with internal affairs and with the Allied intervention, but this last soon came to be closely bound up with the fate of Turkey. The other two, Italy and Greece, both presented claims founded on historical or ethnic grounds, or on promises made in secret agreements during the war.

The effect of these secret agreements was to some extent diminished by President Wilson's refusal to consider them binding, but they none the less greatly influenced the post-war settlement in the Middle East. The fate of Constantinople and

---

[1] "Syria" in 1919 included all of the countries now called Syria, Lebanon, Jordan and Israel, but for convenience the names given to the subsequent divisions of the country are used here.

[2] Kirk, G., *A Short History of the Middle East*, p. 284. Methuen, 1948.

the Bosphorus was left undecided after the Bolshevik revolution
and the consequent lapse of the agreement of 18 March 1915
assigning the area to Russia. The pact of St. Jean de Maurienne,
negotiated in April, and finally agreed on 18 August 1917, by
which Italy was promised extensive territory in Anatolia, was
never formally ratified since it was made subject to Russian
approval. The Sykes-Picot agreement of 16 May 1916, dividing
Syria and Iraq into French and British spheres of influence, lost
much of its importance with Wilson's increasing interest in the
Middle East, and with the development of British governmental
relations with the Zionists. But the growth of Arab nationalism
and of Zionism during the war, and British relations with both,
had enduring consequences for the Middle East and for Britain's
position in that region.

By the end of the war Britain's successful leadership of the
Arab revolt against the Ottomans had given her a dominant
voice in Arab counsels. She had won that leadership partly
through the devoted work of men such as T. E. Lawrence, and
partly as a result of undertakings to assist the Arabs towards
independence after the war. The terms of those undertakings
were not precise either as to the areas of Arab independence
or as to the extent to which British assistance would play a part
in Arab governments. At the same time leading British statesmen, of whom Balfour was the most important, were becoming
steadily more interested in the Zionist movement, primarily
through genuine sympathy with the Zionist cause, but also
through the recognition that close relations with an expanding
Jewish community in Palestine were likely to be beneficial to
Britain's position in the Middle East. Britain's attitude to the
Zionists was officially formulated in the so-called Balfour Declaration—a statement by the British Foreign Secretary in a
letter to Lord Rothschild dated 2 November 1917 to the effect
that "His Majesty's Government view with favour the establishment in Palestine of a National Home for the Jewish people,
and will use their best endeavours to facilitate the achievement
of this object, it being clearly understood that nothing shall be
done which may prejudice the civil and religious rights of the
existing non-Jewish communities in Palestine or the rights and
political status enjoyed by Jews in any other country."[1]

[1] Weizmann, C., *Trial and Error*, p. 262. Hamilton, 1949.

These, then, were the factors that Britain's post-war policy in the Middle East had to take into account: the undertaking to encourage the establishment of a Jewish National Home in Palestine; the promises of independence to the Arabs in areas whose definition was in dispute; the French dislike of a policy of independence for any Arab states and belief that Britain was using the policy to oust France from the Levant; the territorial aspirations of Italy and Greece; her own imperial interests and concern for lines of communication to India and the Far East; the age-old problem of the Straits, now occupied by British, French and Italian forces after the collapse of Turkey and the Bolshevik renunciation of Russian claims.

In circumstances so complex as these, the development of British policy proceeded slowly. Under British encouragement, the Emir Faisal, son of the Sherif of Mecca who had called out the Arabs in revolt against the Turks, agreed with Dr. Chaim Weizmann to accept a Jewish National Home in Palestine pro-vided that Arab independence as delimited during the war were granted and secured. In November 1919, however, Lloyd George's policies of economy and of rapid demobilization of the British army led him to insist on withdrawing the British garrisons in the northern Arab territories. Faisal agreed to a French garrisoning of the Lebanon and the coastal zone of Syria only with reluctance in view of the known French attitude to the Arab aspirations to independence. At length, in April 1920, the Allies agreed in a Supreme Council meeting at San Remo that France should assume mandates for Syria and the Lebanon, Britain for Iraq, Palestine and Transjordan. With this formal composition of Allied differences, the Treaty of Sèvres was dictated to the Turkish Sultan and accepted by him on 10 August 1920. The Arab mandates were confirmed; Arabia and Armenia were declared independent; East and West Thrace went to Greece; Smyrna and the west of Asia Minor were ceded to Italy; the Straits and the Sea of Marmora were demilitarized and placed under the control of an inter-Allied Commission. The break-up of the Ottoman Empire was com-pleted and the interests of all the parties concerned, except those of the Arabs, were apparently secured.

But in the meantime the power of the Sultan had been attacked from within as well as from without. The standard of revolt had been raised on 19 May 1919 by Mustapha Kemal, a participant in the Young Turk reformist movement of 1908, and one of the victorious commanders at Gallipoli during the war. Kemal had the backing of the army and soon gained popular support in Anatolia. He was able swiftly to consolidate his power in Asia Minor and found a natural ally in the Bolsheviks, then fighting for their lives against Allied intervention on behalf of the Whites. One element of this intervention was the support given to Denikin through the Straits and the Black Sea, and evident community of interest existed between Kemal, endeavouring to regain Turkish independence from the Allies, and the Bolsheviks, endeavouring to save themselves from destruction by the Ally-sponsored Whites. Confident in his hold on the army and the Anatolian peasantry, sustained by his friendly relations with the Bolsheviks, and well aware of the disunity among the Allies, Kemal refused to accept the Treaty of Sèvres and defied the Allies to impose it on him by force.

Dormant rivalries now reappeared. The first military steps against Kemal had been taken by Venizelos of Greece, acting with Allied authority, but primarily under the protection of Lloyd George. Neither Italy nor France had any desire to see the power of Britain's Greek protégés established in Asia Minor, and in March 1921 Italy—sufficiently occupied with the Adriatic and with internal problems—took advantage of the fall of Venizelos to withdraw support from the Greeks and come to an agreement with Kemal. Several months later France also reached an informal agreement which was, however, held in abeyance under pressure from Britain. But in London disagreements among the Allies were now matched by disagreements in the British government itself. Lloyd George was all for a policy of whole-hearted support for the Greeks; Curzon fought for a compromise to avoid an open rupture with Poincaré; Montagu, the Secretary of State for India, authorized the Viceroy to publish the pro-Turkish views of the government of India, an action which caused Montagu's resignation but was held by his supporters to have prevented a Muslim rising in India. The evident disunity, both among the Allies and in Lloyd George's own government, together with the exposed military position of the Greeks, encouraged Kemal to launch a major offensive in the summer of 1922, and the last Greek was driven out of Smyrna on 20 August.

Thus by the autumn of 1922 France and Britain were installed as mandatories in the Arab provinces of the Ottoman Empire, each suspicious of the objects of the other and following opposed policies in the face of underground or open Arab hostility; Italy had withdrawn in disgust, and Greece, Lloyd George's protégé, had been forcibly expelled; the whole of Anatolia was occupied by a victorious Kemal in close association with Soviet Russia; the Turks were now threatening the neutral zone on the Straits and the former Turkish territory in Europe. French and Italian detachments were sent to support the British garrison at Chanak, and on 17 September the British press published a communiqué, inspired by Winston Churchill but not previously seen by Curzon, calling attention to the danger and claiming Dominion support to British resistance. The French and Italians were unwilling to be associated with what they considered a provocative policy, and Canada and South Africa intimated that their consent was not to be taken for granted to policies on which they had not been consulted: the now isolated British garrison at Chanak was accordingly withdrawn under an agreement with Kemal by which the Turks occupied Thrace and Adrianople on 14 October. On the 19th the Conservative party, led by Bonar Law, Curzon, Baldwin and Amery, decided to withdraw from the Coalition, and Lloyd George accordingly resigned.

The complete victory of the Allies over the Ottomans was thus largely nullified by their mutual distrust and suspicion, by the indecision of the British government caused by internal disagreements on policy, and by Kemal's leadership backed by the U.S.S.R. The Treaty of Sèvres was scrapped, and settlement in the Middle East was finally reached in the Treaty of Lausanne on 24 July 1923. After lengthy negotiations, the Allies agreed to the abolition of the Capitulations; Turkish sovereignty was recognized over Anatolia and Eastern Thrace; the Greek and Bulgarian frontiers were demilitarized. No agreement could be reached between Turkey and Britain, as mandatory power for Iraq, over the disposition of Mosul. The territory was eventually assigned to Iraq by a decision of the League of Nations in December 1925, and the Turks in con-

sequence hurriedly signed a new treaty of friendship with the
U.S.S.R. But on the initiative of Prime Minister Baldwin general
conversations were opened with the Turks, and they eventually
led to a treaty between the two countries in June 1926. The
period of strained relations was closed, and a slow progress
towards friendliness began. The disposition of the Sanjaq of
Alexandretta similarly remained in dispute between Turkey
and France, as mandatory for Syria, but this dispute was not
settled until 1939 when the territory was annexed by Turkey
a few weeks after the Franco-Turkish Declaration of Mutual
Assistance of 23 June. But the early destruction of her traditional
—if not wholly constant—policy of maintaining her Middle
Eastern interests through alliance with Turkey caused Britain
to place increased reliance on her influence over the Arabs for
the buttressing of her Middle Eastern position. This reliance
could not but increase France's suspicions, and also brought
about an abandonment of the spirit if not the letter of the
Balfour Declaration and the gradual loss of Jewish goodwill.
Turkey for her part looked first to the Soviet Union for the
defence of her independence, and had not the menace of Germany and Italy brought about a new alliance with the west in
time, that independence might well have been lost when the
Stalinists in Moscow began their expansionist policy after
August 1939.

The British policy of leadership in the Middle East through
friendly alliance with and sponsorship of Arab nationalism had
only limited success because of the strength of Arab resistance
to the mandate system, and because of the Jewish problem:
Arab friendship was slowly won in Transjordan and to a less
extent in Iraq, where promises of independence were eventually
redeemed, but Anglo-Arab hostility in Palestine steadily increased as Nazi and Nazi-inspired persecution of the Jews drove
growing numbers to seek refuge in the National Home. The
depth of Arab hostility or distrust was shown in the 1939-45 war,
when the Jews bent all their efforts to the Allied cause, while
the Arabs half-heartedly contributed or openly opposed. Lloyd
George's personal policy, too, of domination of the Straits
through an International Commission and Greek occupation
of Anatolia not merely failed but recoiled on the head of him-

self and his country: the reversal of policy towards the Straits at Sèvres had persisting consequences up to and after the outbreak of the Second World War.

Since the pre-Christian era states have struggled for mastery over the Straits, the gateway of Europe into Asia and Asia into Europe. In the nineteenth century the chief protagonists in that struggle were Russia, striving for a warm-water port in the Mediterranean and fearing attack on herself through the Black Sea, and Britain, fighting for control of the eastern Levant and the land-bridge to the Far East and fearing Russian naval incursions into the Mediterranean. The conflict centred partly on the decaying Ottoman Empire, and partly on the regulations that should govern the passage of vessels through the Straits. In the former issue Russian policy wavered between destroying Turkey and establishing a protectorate over her; British policy in the early part of the century endeavoured to preserve Turkish power, but later favoured the emergence of new national states out of the Ottoman Empire, thus permitting Germany to move into the position of Turkish protector. In the latter question, the traditional Russian aim was for a régime over the Straits which permitted the passage of her own and Turkish warships through the Straits but none others; if she could not gain this optimum position, then she preferred the Straits to be closed to all warships. She thus laid greater stress on defence (prevention of other powers' naval ingress into the Black Sea) than on offence (permitting her own egress from the Black Sea). Britain maintained resolute opposition to restricted naval passage for Russian and Turkish vessels only, but she too preferred a defensive position (no egress for the Russians and no ingress for herself) and thus pressed for prohibition of passage for the naval vessels of all powers.

In order to ensure the continued participation of Russia in the war, Britain had accepted the 1915 Constantinople agreement destining the Straits to Russia. The renunciation of the benefit of this treaty by the Bolsheviks left the disposition of the Straits undetermined. The proposal first canvassed that the United States should become mandatory power for the area was rejected by Washington, and the granting of a mandate to any other single power was clearly impossible because of the rivalries among the Allies. Accordingly, the dictated Treaty of Sèvres placed the Straits under the control of an international commission. The natural corollary of this policy was demilitarization and the opening of the Straits to unrestricted navigation to all vessels in peace or war. Britain was wholly willing to accept this reversal of her traditional position since in 1920 she occupied a dominant position and had recently been able to use that position to forward her assistance to the Whites in southern Russia. Point was given to this experienced advantage by the Turkish closure of the Straits during the war which had led to the costly and unsuccessful Dardanelles campaign having among its objects the opening of southern communications with Russia. But complete freedom of passage was the traditionally least desirable settlement for Russia. It was also distasteful for Turkey in the severe restrictions, albeit international, that it imposed on her sovereignty.

The customary Anglo-Russian conflict thus reappeared at the conference of Lausanne in 1923. Britain, desirous of maintaining her position in the international régime on the Straits, and not at this date fearing a Soviet fleet in the Levant, insisted on free passage in peace or war for all vessels: in this policy she received tepid support from France, in conformity with the latter country's anti-Bolshevik outlook. Chicherin, following in the footsteps of Gorchakov, Izvolsky and Sazonov, fought to have the Straits closed to all warships in peace time. Turkey held the decisive vote, and the temptation to take the Soviet view was strong not merely in the interest of maintaining friendly relations, but because closure of the Straits was likely to entail some reassertion of Turkish sovereignty over them. But for reasons not yet clearly established[1] Turkey took the British side, and the Lausanne convention accordingly confirmed the freedom principle and the demilitarization of the Straits under control of an international commission, while making a small concession to the Soviet view by declaring that no one power should send into the Black Sea a fleet greater than that of any riparian power. This convention the Soviet government refused to ratify.

[1] Three suggested explanations of the Turkish attitude are that she did not like too close an association with and dependence on the U.S.S.R., that she was desirous if possible of re-insuring her position with the west, and that she was fairly confident of the necessity of her friendship to the U.S.S.R. whatever she did. The attitude adopted during the negotiations by Ismet Pasha, leader of the Turkish delegation, suggests that the first, skilfully played on by Curzon, was the governing factor. See Comd. 1814, 1923. *Lausanne Conference on Near Eastern Affairs, 1922-1923.*

In the thirteen years following Lausanne, Britain's relations with Turkey, aided by a succession of able ambassadors in Ankara, steadily improved. The maintenance of good relations with the Soviet Union remained a cardinal principle of Turkish policy, but at the same time Kemal and his Foreign Minister Rüstü Aras cultivated the friendship of Balkan countries closely associated with Britain and France. The difficulties of her position between the Soviet Union on the one hand and Britain and France on the other were greatly relieved by the entry of the U.S.S.R. into the League in 1934 and the latter's signature of the Franco-Soviet pact on 2 May 1935. Turkey could now confidently hope for both Soviet and Anglo-French support against the evidently developing threat to the Levant from Italy, and to a less obvious extent, Germany. On 10 April 1936 Turkey accordingly sent a note to the powers concerned drawing attention to the dangers revealed by the failure of sanctions against Italy and by the German remilitarization of the Rhineland, and requesting a revision of the Lausanne Straits convention.

At the ensuing conference at Montreux Britain had little diplomatic bargaining power with which to resist the traditional pressure from Moscow for a privileged position on the Straits. Some revision was necessary in view of the Italo-German threat, and the U.S.S.R. was now the ally of France and the leading exponent of collective security at Geneva as well as a good neighbour of Turkey. The Montreux convention of 20 July revised Lausanne in two major respects: effective control of the Straits was transferred from the international commission to Turkey, who was authorized to remilitarize them and close them if she were a belligerent; secondly, while the freedom principle was reaffirmed, the *total* of naval tonnage of non-riparian powers in the Black Sea was not to exceed the fleet of any one riparian power, and was not to stay longer than twenty-one days. Thus the Lausanne loophole by which a number of powers acting together could control the Black Sea by combined naval action was effectively closed, and under Montreux the Russians won their hundred years' fight for unlimited egress for herself (unless Turkey were belligerent against her), and controlled ingress for others.

The freedom of passage principle was perhaps less dangerous

to Britain with the twentieth-century's development of air power and the submarine, but the principle could be wholly satisfactory only when the U.S.S.R. was very weak or when she was an ally. When Prime Minister Chamberlain at length decided after the German occupation of Prague in March 1939 that the Nazi threat was real, among his first concerns was to strengthen Britain's position on the Straits. Hence the Anglo-Turkish and Franco-Turkish Mutual Assistance Declarations of 12 May and 23 June respectively. The reversal of the Soviet policy of co-operation against, to co-operation with, aggression, marked by her signature of the pact with the Nazis in August 1939, naturally fundamentally affected her relations with Turkey. She now felt strong enough to abandon the policy of friendship with an independent Turkey and to adopt the policy at one time attempted by Tsar Nicholas I of establishing suzerainty over Turkey. This change in attitude the Turkish Foreign Minister Sarajoglu swiftly found when he visited Moscow in September and October, and the tripartite pact of 19 October with Britain and France, which formalized the mid-summer declarations, lacked the hoped-for support of the U.S.S.R. The reservation contained in a protocol annexed to the pact that its terms should never involve Turkey in war with the Soviet Union was due no longer to their friendly relations, but to the facts of geography and power. The full flowering of the new Soviet policy appeared in Molotov's demand in Berlin in November 1940 for "effective guarantees" not merely "paper guarantees" of her security, a demand defined in his memorandum of 25 November as the establishment of land and naval bases for the U.S.S.R. within range of the Bosphorus and the Dardanelles.[1]

The new Anglo-French alliance with Turkey thus acquired an anti-Soviet character, and the wheel had come full circle. Britain, with the support of France, had reappeared in her traditional nineteenth-century role of endeavouring to preserve an independent Turkey's command of the Straits against the defensive-expansionist pressure from Moscow for a Russian protectorate. The role had originally been abandoned in recognition of Ottoman weakness and as a result of the threat of

[1] *Nazi-Soviet Relations, 1939-1941*, pp. 252 and 258. Department of State, Washington, 1948.

imperial Germany, together with changed strategic assumptions in London. The change led first to the Triple Entente, and then in the war itself to the Constantinople agreement. The collapse of both Turkey and Russia had enabled the Allies for a short period to dominate the Straits, and Britain thus found the principle of freedom of passage in her interest. But when the diplomatic scene shifted, when a new Turkey and a new Russia regained their strength, and the latter again joined in alliance with France against a revived German menace, the new masters in the Kremlin were able to turn Britain's change of policy to their own advantage. In consequence the U.S.S.R. held in 1939 a legal position of power in the Black Sea and of privileged passage through the Straits that the Tsars in the past had never succeeded in obtaining in face of the opposition of Britain.

Chapter 5

THE SOVIET UNION

THROUGHOUT THE nineteenth century Russia had seemed to offer the greatest threat to Britain's interests. British statesmen distrusted Russian activity in the Far East, feared Russian probings towards India, Afghanistan and Persia, fought against Russian attempts to control Turkey and the Straits. But Japan's defeat of Russia in 1904-5 destroyed false notions of Russia's mammoth strength and removed British fears of Russia in the Far East, while at the same time the pressure of German expansionism was increasing both in that region and in Turkey, now no longer supported by Britain. So in 1907 France was able to bring about an uneasy reconciliation of Britain and Russia, their clashing interests in Persia being delimited by agreement on spheres of influence for each. Britain and Russia thus found themselves in 1914 Allies in war for the first time since the defeat of Napoleon.

This collaboration was brought to an end by the two Russian revolutions of 1917. As a military power Russia ceased to exist. The Bolsheviks promised peace and agrarian reform, and the Russian army rapidly disintegrated as its peasant recruits filtered home to participate in the seizures of land that were taking place all over the country. Chaos reigned in government and administration. On 27 November 1917 the British ambassador, Sir George Buchanan, cabled to London that the situation was desperate and that Russia should be released from her obligations and permitted to make a separate peace. The need was, however, already too urgent for delay, and on 28 November the Bolsheviks and the Germans concluded an armistice. At a meeting on 2 December the two parties agreed to a ten days' truce.

The Bolsheviks could not anticipate lenient treatment from the Germans, and they could expect little sympathy from the Allies after their conclusion of an unauthorized armistice. Their only potential strength lay in a call to revolution elsewhere, and this they exploited vigorously, first by beginning the publication and renouncing the benefits of secret treaties found in the Tsarist archives, secondly by appealing to the Allies to join their peace negotiations, and thirdly by calling on all the armies engaged in the war to join the Russian revolution. The Allies failed to respond, the revolutions did not appear, and the Bolsheviks were forced to accept the crushing terms of Brest Litovsk on 3 March 1918.

This treaty was a source of dismay to the Allies, not merely because it formally ended operations on the eastern front, but because it admitted the German armies deep into the Ukrainian granaries. Military opinion insisted on the necessity of operations in the east, but the political situation was one of extraordinary complexity. The titular government of Russia was composed of unknown personalities of unpredictable quality, mouthing phrases of unmeasurable menace. Numerous sects within Russia expressed bitter hostility to this government—peasant groups (right and later also left Social Revolutionaries), Social democratic groups (the Mensheviks), aristocratic constitutional monarchists (the Cadets) and most of the army officers. The chaos in Russia was being exploited to their economic advantage by the militarist government of Germany with which the Allies were at war. Allied forces were sent to Russia to oppose the German armies: on a few occasions they received Bolshevik support, but in general assistance from Russians came from anti-Bolshevik groups. This, then, was the birth of the intervention policy, originally inspired primarily by military considerations.

These same considerations were largely responsible for the continuation of the policy after the German collapse in November 1918, for the new republican government of Germany soon proved itself either unable or unwilling to control its own military leaders, some of whom aimed at compensating for the German defeat in the west by establishing a German-controlled government in the east. Allied intervention in Russia thus began in order to reopen the eastern front against Germany, and it was maintained through 1919 partly, it is true, because of genuine dislike of the Bolsheviks (who were continuing their hostile propaganda, and had repudiated all Russia's foreign debts on 8 February 1918), but primarily to prevent a defeat of the Bolsheviks by the Russian Whites under German and not Allied sponsorship. At times the situation was so confused that Curzon admitted his inability to formulate any general principles of policy at all. But in the making of such policy as there was, the coalition government was as divided as it had been over Mustapha Kemal: the Conservatives, in this instance led by Churchill, were all for major intervention in order to destroy the Bolsheviks; Lloyd George was not merely unwilling to face the cost of such an undertaking, but feared lest the policy should provoke mutinies in the army and labour unrest at home. Once the German danger had been removed, he wished to end intervention and leave the situation to settle itself. Disagreements on policy and objectives, and the general desire to avoid any major military commitment, made intervention indecisive and tentative; in this apparently classic illustration of the Soviet dogma that the capitalists would be bound to combine to destroy the first proletarian state, there was in reality nothing but disunity. France wished to destroy the Bolsheviks; the German military leaders wished to control Russia either through agreement with and domination of the Bolsheviks, or through the establishment of some other government under their own control; Britain was divided within itself; the United States opposed intervention, but participated in Siberia in order to check Japanese imperialism. By the spring of 1920 the Bolsheviks had succeeded in defeating all their enemies, and a renewed French-supported effort by Wrangel in the south swiftly collapsed. During the Russo-Polish War in 1920 interventionist groups in Britain pressed for aid to the Poles, but Lloyd George was able to avoid any such action largely because of the popular support for his attitude won by the successful agitation of councils of action organized for this purpose by the Labour party under Arthur Henderson's guidance.

As in the case of Turkey, then, the British government's participation in the Allied policy of ill-treating an enemy by halves left an evil legacy for their successors, but in the Russian instance the roots of conflict in the Far East, in the Middle East and in the Straits, went far deeper, and they were now fed by the disruptive ideology which the new rulers of Russia professed. The

Conservatives, the traditional defenders of the Empire, remained bitterly hostile to the Bolsheviks and deeply suspicious of their actions and intentions; Lloyd George hoped to make them less intransigent through paths of economic co-operation; the Labour party, led by Ramsay MacDonald, saw the new Russia through mists of idealistic and romantic illusion and pressed for her earliest acceptance within the family of nations. The fluctuations of British domestic politics were therefore reflected in her relations with the U.S.S.R. to a greater degree than in any other field of foreign policy.

Lloyd George's policy of approach through economic channels achieved its one major success in the conclusion of a trade agreement on 16 March 1921 in which each country agreed to abstain from propaganda against the other (neither did); but the problem of liability for Tsarist debts was left for consideration as part of a general settlement. This latter was Lloyd George's prime aim at the Genoa conference in 1922.[1] But deadlock was reached on the Allied claims on Russia for some recognition of Tsarist debts and for compensation for nationalized property, countered by the Soviet demand for compensation for damage done by the Allied intervention during the civil war; and Lloyd George's method of holding these conversations secretly in his villa frightened the German Foreign Minister, Rathenau, into yielding to the pressure of members of his own delegation to enter into friendly relations with the Soviet Union. The treaty of Rapallo of 16 April in effect sealed the fate of the Genoa conference, the chief accomplishment of which was thus to facilitate the formation of that very alliance to which Lloyd George had long feared Germany would be driven by a harsh Allied policy.

The failure of Genoa brought Lloyd George one step nearer to his fall in October, and with the advent to power of a Conservative government, the tone of Anglo-Soviet relations steadily worsened. Violent controversy developed over the execution in Russia of a Roman Catholic priest named Butkevich, the climax being reached in an ultimatum from Curzon on 8 May 1923 demanding the withdrawal of the Russian notes on the Butkevich issue and the cessation of Bolshevik propaganda, especially in the Middle East. The U.S.S.R., having no desire to face a rupture

[1] See Chapter 3, pp. 39–40.

with Britain (the most suitable country from which to import the capital equipment she so urgently needed), sent a conciliatory reply which, after pressure in the House of Commons, was accepted by the government. The trade treaty thus remained in force, but the incident had bared the knife-edge upon which Anglo-Soviet relations were balanced.

Over the next ten years relations fluctuated between uneasy co-operation and open hostility. On 1 February 1924 the first Labour government of Ramsay MacDonald recognized the Soviet government *de jure*, and on 10 August, after arduous negotiations more than once on the point of rupture, two treaties were initialled—a new commercial treaty, and a general treaty in which the Soviet government accepted the principle of compensation, the amount to be determined by a special commission after which the British government would guarantee a loan. But in the November general election the MacDonald government was defeated (probably largely as a result of the Zinoviev letter),[1] and in view of this apparent evidence of Soviet intrigue the new Foreign Secretary, Austen Chamberlain, refused to recommend the draft treaties to Parliament, and they were accordingly never ratified. The renewed strain in Anglo-Soviet relations was intensified by the offer of financial assistance, ostensibly from Russian workers, to the Trades Union Congress during the general strike of 1926 (an offer that was accepted by the miners, but not by the Congress), and despite a steady expansion of trade between the two countries, British financial houses remained unwilling to grant the credits that the U.S.S.R. needed. On 12 May 1927 a British police raid on the headquarters of the Soviet trading organization, Arcos, revealed documents confirming the direction of espionage and subversive activity from the Soviet embassy,[2] and the repercussions of this raid led to the severing of diplomatic relations on 26 May. British exports to the U.S.S.R. slumped from £36 million in 1925 to £11 million in 1928. In December 1929 the second MacDonald

[1] The famous Zinoviev letter purported to be an instruction from the President of the Comintern for the disruption of the British economy and the suborning of the British army. Whether it was genuine or not may never be conclusively proved, but the strong probability is that the letter was a forgery. Its publication at that time served effectively to discredit a policy of *rapprochement* with the Soviet Union.
[2] Soviet supporters claimed that the documents were planted, and that espionage is a function of all embassies. It was, however, the subversive character of the activities described in the documents that caused the violence of the reaction.

government reopened relations and a new treaty was concluded in the following April, but relations once again approached breaking-point with the unco-operative Soviet trading policy during the World Economic Crisis, and in March 1933 with the Russian arrest on charges of sabotage of a number of British engineers working for Metro-Vickers in the Soviet Union. The sentencing of two of them led to a British trade embargo and a Soviet counter-embargo, but in July 1933 emotions cooled on both sides, the convicted engineers were released and expelled from Russia, and the two embargoes were lifted. On 16 February 1934 a new trade agreement was concluded, and thenceforward, under the shadow of Hitler, the threat of a rupture on the slightest pretext receded, although relations remained cold and continued to be marked by suspicion and distrust on both sides.

What were the causes of this mutual dislike and fear? They are to be found partly in the internal affairs of both countries, partly in the activities of the Comintern and the ideological motivation of Soviet policy, partly in clashes of interests in traditional fields of Anglo-Russian conflict. The later development of Ramsay MacDonald and the Labour party has caused to be forgotten the apparent magnitude of the latent threat to British institutions presented by Bolshevik activity. The Labour party had indeed supported the war against Germany, but almost every European participant in the war had experienced serious internal unrest either before or after the armistice. Still more was this true of colonial or semi-colonial peoples. In Britain the councils of action in 1920 had an ominous appearance, and internal conflict reached its highest pitch during the general strike of 1926. The Labour party was itself a comparatively new political phenomenon, and it was perhaps difficult for the defenders of the established order to realize that, despite the evident powerful attraction of the Soviet revolution for the British workers, their objects and those of their leaders were in fact fundamentally different from those of their Russian comrades—indeed the Labour leaders themselves only slowly and reluctantly came to recognize that the Soviet object and method were not their own. British policy towards the U.S.S.R., then, was guided not so much by rational judgment as by emotion—fear on the part of the Conservatives, and nostalgic illusion among the Labourites. The Conservatives' fear had grounds in so far as it perceived threats to British imperial or foreign interests, but was baseless in so far as it thought Labour to be treading the same path as the Bolsheviks. The Labour illusion gradually faded, particularly among the Trade Union elements of the party, but it received a considerable fillip from the Soviet Popular Front policy in the 'thirties. Truck with the Bolsheviks thus seemed to the Conservatives to be furthering both the disruption of the Empire and the advance of dangerous men at home: blind hostility to the U.S.S.R. seemed to the Labour party to be deliberate bogey-building to keep themselves out of power.

Support for each view of the U.S.S.R. was to be found in the actions of the Soviet government at various times in the inter-war period. This inconsistency of Soviet policy resulted partly from the conflict between the needs of the Comintern and those of the Soviet state, partly from personal and factional struggle within the Soviet Union, partly from internal shifts of policy, partly from the ebb and flow of doctrinal controversy. Thus the early period of War Communism, of open revolutionary ac-tivity in the first flush of victory, gave way to the New Economic Policy, necessitated by the shattering of the Russian economy in revolution and civil war; this in turn, after Stalin's elimina-tion first of Trotsky and Zinoviev and then of Bukharin, changed to the ruthless industrialization and collectivization of agricul-ture internally and vigorous prosecution of revolution externally in the period of the first five-year plan and the World Economic Crisis; thirdly came the defensive shift to collective security and the Popular Front to meet the danger of Hitler and Japan, and consolidate Stalinism and economic recovery. These shifts and changes in Soviet policy could not but increase the doubts of those already suspicious, and disconcert those favourably in-clined: they made impossible adequate explanation of Soviet policy except in terms of Marxist-Leninist ideology. Such an explanation could not but increase the evident tension in Anglo-Soviet relations.

However much the reality might be masked on suitable oc-casions by public speeches from Soviet statesmen, Marxism-Leninism in fact denied the possibility of lengthy co-existence of capitalist and "proletarian" states in peaceful relationships. The internal and external situation might require tactical shifts or reversals of policy to exploit favourable conditions or stave off pressing dangers, but in the long run the only way of preserving the Soviet Union from attack was by making the rest of the world Communist also. Stalin therefore favoured the cause of "world revolution" as much as Trotsky—their difference was one of timing and method, not of aim. But the promotion of revolution elsewhere meant the fomenting of internal discontents both in the capitalist countries themselves and in their imperial dependencies. Lenin recognized that after the favourable revolutionary conditions of 1919-21 had ended, the most promising prospects for Comintern activity were in colonial and semi-colonial territories; and Britain, as the largest world colonial power, was naturally the chief target of such activities. On the other hand Britain, as Europe's largest exporter, was the most suitable country from which the Soviet Union could buy its urgently needed capital goods, and the U.S.S.R. equally was a convenient source for many of the raw materials that Britain required. In these circumstances it is perhaps understandable that British relations with the Soviet Union were more strained and unstable than those of any other country: the United States, secure in its geographical isolation and lacking colonial possessions, did not open relations until 1933; relations with European powers other than Britain were at times good when the diplomatic situation was favourable; with Britain open or underground hostility in varying degrees of intensity persisted throughout the period.

The clash of British and Soviet policies manifested itself in the pre-1907 areas of Anglo-Russian rivalry—the Far East, the Middle East and (as we have seen) Turkey. The nationalist or Kuomintang movement in China in the 'twenties aimed primarily at the abolition of foreign privileges and the destruction of foreign influence in China. Britain, as the power with the largest commercial stakes in China, was necessarily a main object of hostility. But the Kuomintang was in large measure organized by two Bolsheviks, Borodin, as political adviser, and Galen, as military adviser. Naturally many in Britain regarded the Kuomintang with fear and hostility, both because of its own objects, and because they feared its success might mean a

Bolshevik domination of China. Britain's position was only saved by Chiang Kai-shek's expulsion of the Bolsheviks from the Kuomintang in 1927, and by the understanding and tactful policy of Sir Austen Chamberlain from December 1926 onwards.[1]

Similarly both Afghanistan and Persia saw Anglo-Soviet struggles for the establishment of a controlling influence in their territory. In both Moscow had some success. Persia in particular, under British protection in 1919 and used as a base for intervention in the Russian civil war, gladly welcomed Soviet troops as liberators when the British withdrew after the defeat of the Russian White general Denikin. The Bolsheviks had not yet abandoned their early idealism, and the Soviet-Persian treaty of 26 February 1921 established excellent relations between the two countries. With Afghanistan, too, after a period of uneasy relations and occasional armed clashes, a treaty was signed on 31 August 1926 and was followed by a period of harmonious association. But in 1929 Amanullah, the Afghan King who had concluded the treaty, fell from power as a result, Soviet leaders asserted, of British intrigue, and British influence thereafter gained ground. Equally in Persia the anti-Communist policy of Reza Shah slowly countered the effects of the high level of economic intercourse between his country and the U.S.S.R., so that by 1940 Molotov was willing to agree with Hitler that the Soviet Union's natural field of expansion was through Persia to the Persian gulf. It was in the Middle East that were fought the main battles of the propaganda war between Britain and the U.S.S.R. which ostensibly formed the major cause of dispute between them.

This, then, was the background against which the Anglo-Soviet negotiations in the summer of 1939 must be viewed.[2] In Britain suspicion of Soviet intentions persisted to that date, particularly among British Conservatives. For the U.S.S.R. new grounds for distrust had been furnished by British policy towards Japan in Manchuria and China, and towards the Fascists and the Nazis in Abyssinia, in Spain, in Austria, but above all at Munich. In part the conflict between the two powers derived from their historical clash of interests in traditional parts of the world. Much more was it due to the fact that, with the United States withdrawn into isolation, Britain was the most powerful

[1] See Chapter 6, pp. 75-77.   [2] See Chapter 12, pp. 154-161.

defender of the capitalist order with interests all over the world, while the ultimate object of Soviet policy, pursued with messianic zeal and with complete disregard for bourgeois standards of morality and of international conduct, was to involve that order in world-wide ruin.

THE UNITED STATES, NAVAL DISARMAMENT AND THE FAR EAST TO 1931

UNITED STATES policy had an importance for Britain greater than that of any other foreign power. Particularly was this the case when military obligations were involved. Thus when the United States guarantee to France was cancelled with the Senate's rejection of the Versailles treaty and the League Covenant, Britain lost little time in withdrawing her own guarantee also. Naturally, therefore, the swing of the pendulum in the United States against Wilsonian idealism and international co-operation fundamentally affected Britain's attitude both to the League and to European problems. The whole reparations and war debts controversy, to take only one example, was governed ultimately by the attitude of the United States. Administration, Congress and public opinion were united in their unwillingness to consider substantial abatement of the war debt obligations of the Allies, particularly of those among them such as Britain who were judged fully capable of bearing the burden of payment. "They hired the money, didn't they?" as Calvin Coolidge is reported to have put it, fairly expressed the American attitude. But Britain, not unnaturally, wished at least to meet her own liabilities to the United States out of the amounts she herself received in reparations from Germany and in repayment of war loans to the Allies, so that the, in European eyes, unsympathetic approach of the United States to the matter of European, and particularly British, debts to herself was largely responsible for maintaining the whole economically distorting system. Even United States membership of the Dawes committee was carefully defined, as has been seen, to avoid any commitment of the United States government, while the early efforts of Harding's administration not to lose possible benefit from the League's technical agencies while at the same time escaping contamination by official contact with them, at times bordered upon the ridiculous.

The area in which the United States showed herself least unwilling to accept foreign commitments was the Far East. Her important trading connections with Japan, her tradition of cultural association with China, and her possession of the Philippines meant that she could hardly remain indifferent to the unsettled conditions there prevailing after the war. But real danger existed of a conflict of policy with Britain. The steady growth of Japanese power—marked by the victory over China in 1894-5, the defeat of Russia in 1904-5, and the Twenty-one Demands on China in 1915—had been watched by the United States with increasing concern. Britain, on the other hand, had been the ally of Japan since 1902, and under the shield of this alliance her interests in the Far East had been effectively safe-guarded. Opinions among members of the Commonwealth as to the value of the alliance were, however, divided. Canada, like the United States a Pacific power, also disliked the evidences of a nascent Japanese imperialism, and favoured bringing the alliance to an end. Premier Hughes of Australia, on the other hand, considered that Japan was less dangerous as an ally than an enemy. In London it was recognized that the alliance had less value than hitherto—of the European powers whose expansion in the Far East Britain had feared, Russia had been defeated in 1904-5 and had fallen into chaos in 1917, and Germany had been destroyed in 1918. Moreover a naval race with the United States resulting from an opposed Far Eastern policy was unthinkable. None the less the tradition and the remembered benefits of the Anglo-Japanese alliance remained strong.

In these circumstances tentative *pourparlers* began in London and Washington. It soon became apparent that the United States wanted to minimize dangers in the Far East through a disarmament conference and through the lapsing of the Anglo-Japanese alliance at its expiry date in 1922, while Britain, though willing to make the major concession of accepting naval parity with another power, desired to maintain the alliance in existence, with the incorporation of a specific exemption of the United States from its application. The question became of urgent importance in London at the beginning of July 1921 when a number of Parliamentary questions were put down about rumours on the future of the alliance circulating after a Dominion Prime Ministers' conference at which the Canadian Premier, Meighen, was believed to have demanded that the alliance should be allowed to lapse. Consideration was accordingly given to proposing to Washington a conference in London on Far Eastern questions. At precisely the same time the United States was considering proposing to Britain a conference in Washington on disarmament. With the encouragement of Harvey, United States ambassador in London, Harding risked public rebuff by cabling London on 10 July suggesting a Washington conference both on disarmament and on the Far East, and by publishing his telegram on the next day. The invitation was by no means wholly welcome in London, for the venue of the conference carried some implication that American wishes with regard to the alliance were likely to prevail, but an open breach resulting from refusal of the invitation could not be contemplated. France soon showed herself willing to attend a conference, though expecting little results in disarmament in view of Anglo-Japanese and United States-Japanese relations. Japan reluctantly agreed to participate only because she feared an outright refusal would leave her in a position of complete isolation, and her reluctance was signalized by the protracted discussions on the agenda during which Britain loyally consulted with her according to the terms of the alliance. Eventually, however, the programme of the United States Secretary of State, Charles E. Hughes, was largely accepted. The conference opened at Washington on 12 November 1921 and dispersed on 6 February 1922.

The agreements reached at the Washington conference decisively affected the evolution of the Far East in the inter-war period, and showed the United States attempting in the Pacific, with British support, that very stabilization of the *status quo* against a potentially expansionist power to which she and Britain refused to commit themselves in Europe. In one fundamental respect, however, the situation in the Far East differed from that in Europe. In the latter region the power of France, who desired to maintain the 1919 settlement, was much less than the potential power of the leading dissatisfied country, Germany. In the Pacific, on the other hand, the two satisfied powers, Britain and the United States, were possessed of much greater strength than the potentially expansionist country, Japan. Secure in her knowledge of ultimate superiority, the United States, with the full accord of Britain, was prepared to conclude agreements involving concessions to Japan and an element of risk, concessions such as France, in her relations with Germany, never felt able to make.

Three major treaties emerged from the conference. The first, the four-power pact of 13 December, was offered by the United States to Japan as a substitute for the jettisoned Anglo-Japanese alliance. The United States thereby participated in a regional consultative agreement, and considerable Senate opposition to an "entangling alliance" was only overcome by the pressure of Henry Cabot Lodge and Elihu Root. The participation of the United States sufficiently compensated Britain for the ending of the Japanese alliance, and Japan could do little but acquiesce or be isolated. The second major agreement, the five-power naval treaty signed on 6 February 1922, represented the first real step towards disarmament. The signatories agreed that the capital ships in their respective navies should be in the ratio of 5 for Britain and the United States to 3 for Japan to 1·6 for France and Italy. Britain thus made the major concession of accepting naval parity with another power. Its scope was limited to capital ships only, but the restriction was due to divergence of view over cruisers and smaller vessels not between Britain and the United States (though the divergence undoubtedly existed) but to the inability of France to agree to Italy's demand for parity in all classes of vessels. Moreover even this restricted limitation was accepted by Japan only in view of a further understanding that Britain and the United States would construct no naval bases nearer to Japan than their existing bases at Singapore and Hawaii, while she herself would not construct bases on the former German Pacific islands now mandated to her. The United States Secretary of State was wholly willing to exchange a reduction in the offensive power of the Japanese fleet for a relief from the necessity of spending money on the construction of offensive bases nearer Japan, but the effect of the provision was to make the Japanese mainland temporarily almost impregnable from British or United States naval attack. There was evident danger here should Japan resume her expansionist activities.

Third among the major agreements was the nine-power pact, also signed on 6 February, by which the signatories agreed jointly to maintain the *status quo* in the Far East and not to exploit the present disturbed internal conditions of China for their own advantage. This regional agreement supplemented without replacing the Covenant of the League, and thus formed something of a precedent for Locarno, but it had, of course, the great advantage over the Covenant that the United States was numbered among its signatories. Complementary to this treaty, primarily affecting China, Japan agreed to return Shantung to Chinese sovereignty,[1] but retained effective economic control; the powers agreed a new customs treaty permitting China to raise her rates, and promised to investigate the questions of extraterritoriality and tariff autonomy; on 11 February the United States at last recognized the Japanese mandates over the former German islands, and Japan granted the United States cable rights on the island of Yap. The United States did not succeed in bringing intervention in Siberia to a close (it lasted until the end of 1922), and China failed to obtain a Japanese renunciation of the Twenty-one Demands of 1915, but in all other matters the conference seemed to have achieved a re-sounding success.

The French expectation of a naval armaments race between Britain and the United States in view of the relations between Britain and Japan on the one hand and the United States and Japan on the other had been falsified by the moderate and con-ciliatory attitude of both the British and American delegations. The United States renounced any attempt to assert world mari-time leadership, not least because of the financial burden such an attempt would impose. Britain gave up that position of naval supremacy which was traditionally hers and which she had but lately fought a major war partly to preserve: she accepted the principle of parity with the United States in part because she knew the impossibility of matching United States resources should a race be entered upon, and partly because she recog-

---

[1] Wilson's agreement at Paris to the cession by Germany of Shantung to Japan, ostensibly for onward transmission to China, had been a major element in the cam-paign against the treaty and the Covenant. Wilson had only agreed to this breach of the principle of self-determination because of a Japanese threat that otherwise they would not join the League.

nized the value of United States co-operation and friendship. But she thereby substituted the United States for Japan as her partner in Far Eastern affairs, a substitution which weakened her own position for two reasons—first because her interests were Japan's much more than they were those of the United States, and secondly because Japan's successes could not have been achieved without her alliance, whereas her support to the United States was to prove useful, no doubt, but not essential. The administration in Washington was thus able to dictate, if not major decisions of policy, at least the pace at which agreed policies should be pursued. Particularly was this the case during the 'twenties in United States policy towards the Kuomintang, a movement hostile to Britain and organized by Britain's most determined enemies, the Bolsheviks. It was perhaps the major achievement of Sir Austen Chamberlain as Foreign Secretary that in face of this independent and unco-operative American policy, he yet succeeded in saving much of Britain's interests and influence in China.

The defeat of China by Japan in the war of 1894-5 had begun a movement which was to turn China's contempt for the foreigner into a hatred of all alien possession of privileges or rights over Chinese territory or property. The first sign of this change came in the Boxer rebellion of 1900, the second in the revolution that overthrew the Manchu dynasty and created the Chinese republic in 1911-12. One of the two leaders of that revolution, Sun Yat-sen, withdrew and left the field to Yuan Shih-kai, but after the latter's submission to Japan in 1915 and in view of his evident inability to control and unify the country, Sun returned to political activity and began to reorganize the Kuomintang movement in Canton, with administrative and military expert assistance from the Soviet Union. After Sun's death in Peking in March 1925 during discussions between the Peking and Canton administrations, the leadership of the Kuomintang was assumed by its military commander, Chiang Kai-shek, who soon determined to unify China by military force. Accordingly, in July 1926, he began the long march north from Canton. The threat to British interests was obvious. The whole popular foundation of the Kuomintang movement was its anti-foreign nationalism, and Britain held the most valuable and important concessions in all China except Manchuria; the movement was organized by Borodin on Soviet lines under a single party commanded by a dictatorial central committee, and the degree of Communist domination was impossible to determine; Borodin himself endeavoured to give the nationalism of the Kuomintang as anti-British a flavour as possible. The issue of whether or not the attempt should be made to enforce observance of the treaties was swiftly raised with Chiang's imposition without agreement of customs surtaxes on the levels fixed at Washington: the United States minister in China, MacMurray, favoured strong action in defence of the treaties, but his Secretary of State, Kellogg, was willing only to protest, while British policy favoured recognition of the Chinese right to impose the surtaxes since they would be imposed in any case. The direction of British policy was strikingly confirmed first by the accrediting of Miles Lampson (now Lord Killearn) to Chiang's Hankow government on 8 December 1926, and secondly by a policy memorandum of 18 December, amplified by Sir Austen Chamberlain in a speech a few weeks later. This memorandum marked a revolutionary change in British policy towards China and foreshadowed concessions so extensive that even the eventual surrender of Hong Kong seemed not outside the bounds of possibility. The theme of the memorandum was that the powers should no longer assume that China's political and financial prosperity was dependent on foreign support. China should have the right to alter or impose customs duties; her legitimate demands for revision of the treaties should be admitted; the powers' extraterritorial rights should be revised; steps should be taken in due course for the return of certain leased territories.

These forward-looking principles of policy had considerable effect in enabling Chiang Kai-shek and his more moderate supporters within the Kuomintang to defeat and destroy the Bolshevik-inspired elements who aimed to turn the movement into Communist channels and pursue an uncompromisingly anti-imperialist policy. The success of the march north brought into the open the underlying opposition between the Communist aim (a mass revolution officered by a Communist minority) and that of Chiang (a property-owning national-unifying revolution against foreign privileges). Open conflict broke out between the two wings in the early months of 1927 and the

British government felt it necessary to send a defence force to Shanghai to protect British persons and property in the international settlement. Kellogg persisted in his policy of doing nothing that might cause friction with Chiang, and the only protection he offered United States nationals was to provide facilities for their evacuation: in actual fact these facilities did not have to be used since British and Japanese forces defended the settlement against incursions both from the armies supporting Peking and from those of the Kuomintang. On 27 March, however, a number of attacks were made on foreigners and their property in Nanking, and Kellogg agreed with Chamberlain to bring pressure to bear on Chiang in order to strengthen the latter's hand against his own extremists. An unsatisfactory reply was received from Chiang's left-dominated government, now in Hankow, but Kellogg would not accede to the desires of Britain, France, Italy and Japan and his own minister MacMurray to impose sanctions to enforce compensation. No further joint notes were accordingly presented about the Nanking pogrom in order not to reveal disunity among the treaty powers. The United States was the first to make an independent settlement by an exchange of notes on 29 March 1928; Britain followed suit in August; Japan was the last to reach agreement in May 1929. In line with Kellogg's statement of 17 January 1927 that the United States was willing to negotiate independently on tariffs and the treaties with any delegation representative of China, the United States was also the first to grant China tariff autonomy in the summer of 1928, and by 1 February 1929 tariff autonomy had been granted by eleven of the treaty powers. The question of extraterritoriality, due for consideration in 1931, was postponed because of the Japanese invasion of Manchuria, and was only settled in 1943. Meanwhile Chiang had successfully liquidated the Communists within the Kuomintang in the spring and summer of 1927 (they soon reappeared in south Kiangsi), and with the fall of Peking to the Nationalists on 8 June 1928 the Kuomintang government at Nanking received formal recognition from the powers.

In this confused and dangerous situation in China in the middle 'twenties British policy had successfully followed a line at once conciliatory and firm. With minor exceptions British lives and property had been defended, and the great danger presented by the anti-foreign inspiration of the Kuomintang and its Communist direction had been averted. This was made possible partly by the fundamental opposition between Chiang and the Communists, but also by the speed with which Britain, possessor of the greatest stakes in China, had recognized the necessity of conciliation and compromise. With this latter policy the United States administration concurred, but in line with traditional American policy the Secretary of State proved wholly unwilling to participate in military measures for the protection of international, or even American, settlers and their property. Such assistance as Britain received came primarily from her former ally, Japan, and not her new one, the United States. The lessening of Britain's ability to defend her Far Eastern interests as a result of her change of partners, dictated by considerations of global policy, was thus revealed—though this is not, of course, to determine whether Britain would or should have attempted an integral defence of those interests in the post-war world had Japan remained her partner. The adroitness of British policy in China at this time is, however, sufficiently evidenced by her avoidance both of heavy losses of property and perhaps of life (which she and the United States would almost certainly have suffered had the international settlements not been defended by British and Japanese troops), and of the hostility which Japan aroused first by her direct intervention in 1927, and secondly by her dilatory and reluctant yielding of rights and privileges to the conquering Kuomintang government. The nascent good will between the Kuomintang on the one hand and Britain and the United States on the other was, however, to be largely dissipated by the weakness of the two powers in the crisis of 1931.

The second major field of international affairs in which Britain was closely involved with the United States was that of naval disarmament. As has been seen, the agreement reached at Washington marked the co-operative approach of both countries to the problem, but the scope of the ratios agreed had been restricted to capital ships because of the Franco-Italian dispute over parity. But disarmament was a project peculiarly acceptable to the Republican administrations of the 'twenties in the United States. It offered a valuable political platform to which many Americans adhered with genuine idealism; it presented a method of making large reductions in public expenditure; by reducing the offensive strength of all powers, it made the United States' geographical isolation even more secure and permitted the uninterrupted enjoyment of surging prosperity. Dissatisfaction with the restricted character of the Washington five-power treaty mounted in the middle 'twenties, coupled with irritation that Britain was planning a cruiser fleet considerably larger than that of the United States. The Coolidge administration was consequently pressed in 1926 to obtain an agreement on parity between Britain and the United States in all vessels instead of in capital ships only—parity to be achieved of course, by British reductions, not by United States building up to the new British programme. The need for some diplomatic achievement was increased by the fiasco over the admission of the United States to the World Court at the Hague. A United States proposal for a further naval conference was accordingly put forward, and the three leading powers met at Geneva in June 1927. Both France and Italy refused to attend because France remained unwilling to discuss parity with Italy in all classes of vessels, the only basis upon which Italy would send delegates. The conference broke down in complete failure. There was almost no diplomatic preparation for it, and the British and United States delegations found their instructions fundamentally opposed. The defence of British commercial and strategic interests throughout the world demanded a certain minimum number of cruisers below which she would not go: the United States was willing neither to build up nor to fix absolute minima—she wished to establish relative ratios of tonnages on the model of the Washington treaty. Complete deadlock was reached, and the conference closed without agreement.

The advent to power of the second Labour government in Britain in 1929 improved the prospects for a new disarmament agreement, and a period of intensive diplomatic preparation was brought to a climax by the visit of MacDonald to Washington from 4 to 10 October. There he successfully combated traditional United States views about the freedom of the seas and in particular the exemption of food ships from blockade in time of war (a main reason, in President Hoover's view, why peace-time navies had to be so large) and agreement was reached on the difficult cruiser question through a reduction by MacDonald of Britain's minimum cruiser requirements by nearly one third. A new treaty accordingly emerged from the London naval conference on 22 April 1930 in which the five major powers agreed on a holiday in the building of capital ships, and on a limit on the number of submarines and their methods of employment; but no reconciliation of the Franco-Italian conflict was achieved, so only Britain, the United States and Japan signed further clauses laying down a 10:10:7 ratio for cruisers with submarine parity at a low level. The familiar Franco-British divergence over security and disarmament once more reappeared. France did not feel able to contemplate Italian naval superiority in the Mediterranean[1] without a mutual guarantee system modelled on Locarno: Britain disliked the idea of a guarantee in the western Mediterranean only (in contrast to France, Britain's vital interests centred in the Levant rather than the western basin), and would offer none without United States participation. The greatest commitment the United States would consider was a consultative pact, and then only if French security was already guaranteed by a Mediterranean Locarno. No agreement on additional security for France could therefore be reached, and in these circumstances France would not consider halving her navy or encouraging Italy to double hers, which was what near-parity involved. In the months following the London treaty Britain worked intensively on the thankless task of mediation, and was abused by both sides, particularly France, but success was apparently achieved in the bases of agreement of 1 March 1931. Their interpretation caused further contention, however, and French fears of reducing her cruiser strength as provided for in the bases were further enhanced by the open evidence of German naval building. The succeeding naval treaty of London of 25 March 1936 was signed only by Britain, the United States and France, and under its terms the ratio system and quantitative limitation were abandoned, and the three powers (with the later accession of Germany and the Soviet Union) agreed only

---

[1] Italian policy under Mussolini had up to this date cultivated good relations with Britain, but had pursued aims in direct opposition to France both in the Balkans and in North Africa.

to make public declarations of their building programmes, and to accept certain limits on vessel tonnages and gun calibres.

In both these problems in which Britain and the United States were closely involved—the Far East, and naval disarmament—British policy had followed the same general lines as that of the United States, but in both issues the greater power and the greater security of the western hemisphere had enabled the United States to move farther and faster than Britain was prepared to go. Similar factors thus affected the relations of Britain with the United States and of Britain with France, though her roles were reversed in the two cases. In the latter instance she was the desirable but aloof ally, more powerful and less threatened: in the former case, she herself was the weaker partner, and had greater need of the support of her associate. With neither country were her relations consistently harmonious—indeed with both, disagreement and lack of co-operation persistently recurred. These disagreements were inherent in the different situations and histories of the three countries, but they only masked a basic community of interest and purpose. That they sufficed to keep the three countries divided until one was destroyed and a second on the brink of disaster is sufficient commentary on the quality of their statesmen and the self-centredness of their peoples.

Chapter 7

THE MANCHURIAN CRISIS AND THE
SINO-JAPANESE WAR

THE *de jure* recognition of the Kuomintang government at Nanking on 8 June 1928 set the formal seal on the success of Chiang's movement. There remained, however, the problem of Manchuria. This country had not formed part of the ancient empire of China (it lay outside the great wall), but it had a long history of association with China, the closeness of the relationship being symbolized by the Manchu dynasty overthrown in 1911. But through the latter part of the nineteenth century control of Manchuria had been one of the major prizes sought by Russia: in 1896, after Japan's defeat of China in the Sino-Japanese war of 1894-5, Russia had succeeded in obtaining China's consent to the construction in Manchuria of the last section of the Trans-Siberian railway to Vladivostok. The territory through which the railway ran was leased by China to Russia. Japan became seriously alarmed lest Russia's influence should extend not merely through Manchuria, but south into Korea, thus presenting a major threat to Japanese metropolitan territory. Accordingly, after her defeat of Russia in 1904-5, Japan took care to ensure that Russia's influence was pushed back in Manchuria, and she herself extracted from a reluctant China a lease of the territory in south Manchuria in which branches of the Trans-Siberian railway had been constructed. In this way both Russia and Japan came to hold leased railway zones in Manchuria, the Russian known as the Chinese Eastern Railway, and the Japanese as the South Manchuria Railway.

Neither the treaty of Portsmouth which had ended the Russo-Japanese war in September 1905, however, nor the Komura treaty of the following December, had precisely defined the limits of the Japanese monopoly or the Chinese right to construct their own communications. Throughout the troubled

JAPAN,
MANCHURIA
AND CHINA

times in China after 1911 control of Manchuria had been maintained by Chang Tso-lin, Japan's ally in the war against Russia,
and he had been the chief support of Peking's dying resistance to
the Kuomintang in 1927-8. The Kuomintang's task of unifica-
tion remained uncompleted so long as Manchuria lay outside
their control. The anti-foreign inspiration of the movement was
now largely concentrated against Japan, the most unyielding
defender of foreign privileges in China proper, and against the
Soviet Union, as the home of Communism, and these factors
combined to make probable a Kuomintang attempt to overthrow Japan's friend, Chang Tso-lin, and oust Japan and the
U.S.S.R. from their respective railway zones. But on 4 June
1928 Chang was killed by a bomb that exploded under the train

in which he was travelling[1] and his son, Chang Hsueh-liang, soon made a deal with the Kuomintang under which he was recognized as the ruler of Manchuria and in return accepted Nanking's suzerainty.

The Young Marshal's submission to Chiang Kai-shek's régime foreshadowed an early attempt to eject foreign interests from Manchuria, and on 27 May 1929, on the pretext of subversive Communist activity, Chang ordered the arrest of the Soviet manager of the Chinese Eastern Railway, the occupation of the railway zone and the expropriation of Soviet interests. The Soviet government replied with mobilization and an ultimatum in August, and when negotiations with Chang failed, hostilities broke out. A note from Washington calling attention to the Kellogg pact[2] was rejected by Moscow on the ground that the matter was one of self-defence, and on 22 December Chang agreed to restore the Soviet rights in full. He recovered prestige, however, through the valuable assistance he gave to Chiang Kai-shek against a new war-lord uprising in 1930, and he thereafter began a more cautious campaign against the Japanese South Manchuria Railway—by defaulting on loans, by obstructing the development of Japanese business activities, by building new lines parallel to the Japanese tracks, and by planning a new port to compete with Dairen.

Meanwhile a number of influences had been undermining the power of the liberal Minseito governments in Tokyo. Underneath the co-operative foreign policy of Shidehara the latent forces of expansionism remained. The military ambition of the Japanese army, the special constitutional position of the army and the navy giving them an effective veto over any Cabinet, the economic need for markets and raw materials and the belief that only political control would secure them, the hatred of the west, the fear of Communism—all these simmered underground throughout the post-war decade. They were brought to the surface by a combination of circumstances in 1930 and 1931.

[1] The responsibility for the outrage has never been conclusively determined Some believed it to have been Chinese-inspired because of Chang's intrigues with Japan, others that the Japanese were responsible, because Chang had been unwilling to accept the degree of protection that they wished to offer him. The balance of opinion favours the latter hypothesis.

[2] An agreement at first planned for signature by the United States and France, and later signed by sixty-five nations including Britain, by which the signatories renounced the use of war as an instrument of national policy.

The World Economic Crisis brought into disrepute the orthodox financial policy of the Minseito government, and imposed intolerable burdens on the debt-ridden peasantry. The crisis further caused commercial disaster with the failure of the silk trade in face of the prohibitive United States Smoot-Hawley tariff at a time when a Chinese boycott at Shanghai was already seriously damaging Japanese trade. On the other hand the prospects for an adventure were made more favourable by British and American absorption in economic and financial problems, while the Soviet break with Chiang Kai-shek in 1927 and success against the Young Marshal in 1929 made interference from the north less likely and at the same time pointed the danger of an extension of Soviet influence. The London naval treaty aroused bitter naval opposition, over-ruled by Prime Minister Hamaguchi, and the army gained a new ally in its resistance to Shidehara's foreign policy. All these elements of discontent were brought to a focus by Chang Hsueh-liang's campaign against the South Manchuria Railway, evidently aimed at the ejection of Japan from Manchuria. On the night of 18/19 September 1931 occurred the Mukden incident,[1] taken by the Japanese army as a pretext for launching a well-planned and prepared operation by which in the space of a few months the whole of Manchuria was conquered.

The Japanese invasion of Manchuria ranks with the Italian attack on Abyssinia and the German remilitarization of the Rhineland as one of the three decisive actions of the inter-war years. The invasion was the first major military operation undertaken since 1918, and it presented a far more difficult problem than, say, the Greek attack on Bulgaria in 1925, since the state involved was one of the five permanent members of the League Council. Though there was no doubt of the provocation of the Young Marshal, there was nothing in the dispute that could not have been settled by arbitration or recourse to the Hague, and the evidence of planned aggression by the Japanese army was

---

[1] The incident consisted in the blowing up of a small section of the South Manchuria Railway near Mukden. Whether or not the bomb was planted by the Japanese—as was suspected—the army was clearly only waiting for some excuse to launch a planned offensive, and the scale of the incident could not be held to justify a conquest of Manchuria. The damage was so slight that a train passed over the spot only a few hours later.

swiftly conclusive. The Japanese action thus presented the League of Nations with its first real test: the response of the nations assembled at Geneva would determine whether or not collective security existed, and therefore whether the nations could afford to disarm or must rely on their own individual armed strength.

Great Britain held the key position at Geneva. Not only was she the only great power with vital interests in the Far East, but as the strongest naval power in the League and the largest world trader, no sanctionary action, whether economic or military, could be of any effect without her full participation. But in the early stages no strong policy could be expected from London because Britain was in the most acute phase of political and economic crisis: the Labour government fell amid bitter controversy and the National government was formed at the end of August, the so-called mutiny at Invergordon occurred on 15 September, the Mukden incident was on the night of the 18th/19th, Britain went off the gold standard on the 21st, and a general election was fixed for 27 October. While public opinion vaguely and idealistically supported the League, it was inevitable that attention should be monopolized by political and economic developments at home. An initial temporizing policy was not likely to be changed by the Foreign Secretary appointed after the election, Sir John Simon, who was temperamentally disinclined to a strong policy. His personal disinclination received encouragement from suggestions that a collapse of Japan would lead to Soviet dominance in Inner Mongolia, Manchuria and thence China, and that resistance to Japan in China might divert her attention to Britain's even more vital interests in south-east Asia; some of his expert advisers remembered the Anglo-Japanese alliance and the advantages it had conferred on Great Britain; some of the business interests concerned in China not unnaturally sympathized with Japan's action against the Kuomintang's cancelling of foreign privileges—Britain's exports to China in the decade 1920-30 declined from 16·46 per cent to 8·15 per cent of China's total imports.[1] These factors are difficult to assess and should not be exaggerated, but Simon himself believed Japan to be a stabilizing influence and said so at a private Press luncheon in January 1932 at which some Americans were present.

[1] Gull, E. M., *British Economic Interests in the Far East*, p. 111. O.U.P., 1943.

More decisive factors in the shaping of British policy, however, were the attitude of the United States, and economic and strategic considerations affecting British and American policies alike. League action in the economic field could be no more efficacious without United States support than without that of Britain, for no less than a third of Japan's trade was with the United States. The policy of Secretary of State Stimson was guided by three main considerations.[1] Effective naval action against Japan was impossible because of the policies adopted by agreement at Washington in 1921-2. The immediate result of sanctionary action against Japan was likely to be a Japanese blockade of the Chinese coast which could not be broken by naval force, and all trade with both Japan and China would be brought to an end at a time when economic crisis was already acute. These two considerations weighed equally with Simon in London as with Stimson in Washington. But the latter's position was further weakened by the fact that 1932 was a Presidential election year and Hoover was not likely to sanction a strong policy. United States public opinion sympathized with China on account of their long religious and cultural association, but was sure to reject any policy likely to worsen the economic crisis, or any that would involve co-operation with Europe and the League—traditional isolationism being exacerbated at this time by bitterness over the war debt question. At the mid-term elections in 1930 Hoover and Stimson had lost control of Congress, and in December 1931 Congress voted down a proposal for the reduction of war debt obligations. Whatever Stimson's personal views may have been, no strong policy could evidently be expected from Washington. It is unlikely that Britain would have sponsored a strong policy even had United States support been forthcoming, but without that support the smallest chance of effective action disappeared.

The crucial period of the crisis was between September and December 1931. In this period United States policy was the decisive factor. After December diplomatic action continued to be taken, now mainly by the United States with Britain and the

---

[1] His book *The Far Eastern Crisis*, Harper, 1936, is a tendentious account that needs to be compared with Pratt, J. T., *War and Politics in China*, Cape, 1943, or better Smith, S. R., *The Manchurian Crisis 1931-32*, Columbia U.P., 1948.

League apparently reluctantly tagging along, but the issue by then had been in effect already decided. On 19 September the League was informed of the Mukden incident, and on 21 September (the day Britain went off the gold standard) China appealed to the League under Article 11, the general conciliation article. The appeal was followed by a period of intense canvassing behind the scenes. The first proposal was that a neutral investigating commission should be sent to Manchuria: this China accepted provided hostilities were brought to a close and Japanese troops were withdrawn within the South Manchuria Railway zone, but on 23 September Stimson refused United States participation (his argument being that the commission would cause Shidehara to lose face and would weaken his hand against the Japanese army extremists[1]—an argument of a type that was to become very familiar in later years), and Japan refused to agree to the sending of such a commission. A proposal for League conciliation was met from Washington with a preference for direct negotiation between the two parties, and a temporizing resolution was passed by the Council on 30 September calling upon both parties to cease hostilities.

The 30 September resolution having no effect, a renewed and now successful attempt was made to associate a United States representative with Council discussions (Stimson now having realized that the Japanese Cabinet was unable to control the Japanese army and was willing to take advantage of its successes[2],) but, apparently on Hoover's insistence, the instructions to the United States delegate were drawn so narrowly that he was permitted to participate in discussion under the Kellogg pact only, and in fact he spoke only once after his initial remarks defining his position. This limitation of function caused great disappointment to Briand and Cecil, the French and British representatives at Geneva. A series of moderate resolutions calling upon Japan to withdraw into the railway zone in order to enable negotiations to begin were refused by Yoshizawa, the Japanese delegate, apparently contrary to his instructions from Shidehara in Tokyo;[3] and accordingly a stronger resolution was presented on 24 October calling on Japan to withdraw into the

---

[1] Stimson, H. L., *The Far Eastern Crisis*, p. 43.
[2] *Ibid.*, p. 55.
[3] Smith, S. R., *The Manchurian Crisis*, p. 94.

zone by 16 November. Unfortunately Stimson, who describes his policy as acting parallel with the League, sent no notes to Tokyo following the terms of the 30 September or the 24 October resolutions until 5 November, and even then he did not mention the vital 16 November time-limit. This discrepancy could not but have suggested to Japan a lack of co-operation between the United States and the League. The position was not improved by Stimson's decision to attach a special representative to Geneva, for the man he chose, Charles G. Dawes, was ignorant of the issues involved, was friendly with the Japanese, and pursued his own private mediatory policy almost without discussion with the Council or the League powers.

It was evident by 16 November that Japan was neither withdrawing her troops nor intending to do so, and accordingly Dawes was asked informally whether the United States would support a sanctions policy. He was told to reply that the United States administration had no statutory authority with which to put sanctions into force, that Congress was not in session and would not pass the necessary legislation if it were, and that both the Kellogg pact and the nine-power pact relied on the sanction of public opinion, which had the full support of the United States. It is probable that the decision to give so categorical a negative to any idea of sanctions came from the President himself. All possibility of sanctions was now excluded, because they would be valueless without United States support—but this is not, of course, to say that sanctions would have been imposed had a favourable response been received from Washington. Some action was, however, necessary so that the League should not appear to be as impotent as it in fact was, so once again the idea of a neutral investigating commission was canvassed. This Japan was willing to accept, provided the cessation of hostilities was not made a prior condition. After strenuous pressure the Chinese were induced to waive this condition, Japan herself proposed the commission on 21 November, and Assembly approval was given on 10 December. On the following day the government of which Shidehara was a member fell, on the 13th Japan went off the gold standard, and with Yoshizawa at the Foreign Ministry the Japanese army evidently had a free rein.

In this decisive period, then, League policy under British leadership moved with caution and circumspection. The desire to keep Japan in the League, pressing domestic considerations, strategic difficulties—these dictated a hesitant policy; but those who advocated a strong policy found themselves silenced by the even greater caution of the United States administration—refusing to participate in the first proposed neutral commission, opposing Council mediation, narrowly restricting formal co-operation with the Council, belatedly taking parallel action, categorically rejecting any idea of a sanctionary policy. The members of the Lytton commission were only slowly nominated, there was delay over its sailing, and it arrived only in February 1932, the month in which Japan declared the creation of the new independent state of Manchukuo.

Some degree of Anglo-American co-operation had been achieved in their joint participation in the Lytton commission, but this was to be shattered by two developments in January and February. On 7 January Stimson issued a note stating that the United States would not recognize any changes in the Far East accomplished in contravention of the nine-power pact or by methods inconsonant with the Kellogg pact. In the United Kingdom a Foreign Office communiqué to the Press stated that the government had not felt it necessary to send a note similar to that of the United States. The communiqué read as an open rebuff to the United States, and caused fury in Washington and delight in Tokyo. The lack of British concurrence was due to the fact that the proposed note was received in London only on 5 January and there was no time to obtain the agreement of all members of the League, but the form of the communiqué was undoubtedly a capital blunder. Matters were not improved by a misunderstanding in mid-February when Stimson proposed the invocation of the consultation clause of the nine-power pact but understood Simon on the transatlantic telephone to have refused. In fact Simon said (and repeated in a confirmatory note) that that could be considered when Stimson's non-recognition doctrine was accepted by the League (as it was on 16 February),[1] but Stimson, apparently believing Britain had again refused to go along with him, on 23 February published a letter to Senator Borah, chairman of the Senate Foreign Relations committee, with the objects of enlightening American public opinion, warning Japan, and prodding Britain and the

[1] On both these issues see Pratt, J. T., *War and Politics in China*, pp. 226-8.

League along certain suggested lines of action. Britain in turn was angered by this unilateral action, and no further important development occurred until the Lytton commission published its report on 2 October. The report admitted provocation to Japan but denied any justification for the scale of the Japanese action; it called for non-recognition of Manchukuo; it suggested various practical steps that might be taken. But little action could be expected from the United States in the last weeks of a Presidential election, and on 8 November Hoover and his administration were heavily defeated by Roosevelt. There was therefore no effective United States government until March, and by that date France and Britain were deeply concerned over Hitler's accession to power in Germany, and the United States had reached the peak of its financial crisis. On 24 February the League passed a report against Japanese opposition on the lines of the Lytton report, and on 27 March Japan in consequence gave the requisite two years' notice of her intention to leave the League.

The Manchurian crisis demonstrated that the force of world public opinion was powerless to prevent aggressive action by a determined great power. Such action could only be checked by one or more of the other great powers, whether with or without the support of the League, and that meant war. Whether aggression by a great power would be effectively opposed therefore depended upon the degree to which the other great powers considered themselves to be threatened. The League could not by its simple existence prevent war: all it could do was so to organize preparations for war against an aggressor that the consequences of aggression would be necessarily disastrous, and the aggressor would therefore be deterred from acting. It was the policies of the powers, particularly Britain and the United States (dictated as these policies were by very cogent considerations), that caused the failure of the League in 1931-2, but British governmental leaders in the 'thirties drew the conclusion that Manchuria and Abyssinia proved collective security a failure when their own policies had made it so. With the brief interlude of Abyssinia, British governments after Manchuria paid less and less attention to Geneva (despite the efforts of Anthony Eden and a few others), but until 1938 the British electorate was led to believe that their National government gave whole-hearted allegiance to the League ideal. The delusion of the British public about the power of the League as distinct from the power and policies of its members, and about the attitude of their government towards it, was one of the major reasons for the fatal weakness of British policy in the years before 1939.

The revelation of British policy afforded by Manchuria could not but confirm the attitude of France to the questions of security and disarmament. Britain had shown not merely how weak her position was, but had even allowed to appear through the mouth of Simon a certain complacency towards the Japanese action, and an understanding of the grievances causing it, that boded ill for her attitude to France's now resurgent enemy, Germany. After her last attempt at collective security in November 1932, France returned openly to a policy of *blocs* and alliances against Germany, of which the League was the largest but least effective. France's eastern allies also strengthened their mutual ties or, like Poland, moved away from League co-operation and made friends with the new Germany. British relations with the United States, finally, suffered a severe setback after the more co-operative phase since 1929. The unwillingness of Britain to act without United States support was publicly demonstrated, and that support had not initially been forthcoming: on the other hand the myth that Stimson had wished to pursue a strong policy against Japan but Britain had refused to go along with him added fuel to the fire of Anglophobia which was always liable to burn in the United States and which the isolationists were always glad to stoke. In its revelation of British and League weakness and consequent encouragement to other expansionist powers, in the resultant hardening of French policy, and in its effect on Anglo-American relations, the Manchurian crisis registered a heavy defeat for fundamental British policies.

The conquest of Manchuria did not satisfy the Japanese militarists whose control in Tokyo was now practically complete. After a temporary pause in 1932, the Japanese army suddenly swept forward from Manchuria into Jehol early in 1933 and occupied the whole region up to the Great Wall of China. The

Tangku truce, concluded on 31 May, brought a cessation of the fighting, but gave China little respite. The pressure was maintained by the government of Manchukuo, for whose actions the Japanese disclaimed responsibility. On 18 April 1934 a policy statement in Tokyo, known as the Amau declaration, claimed for Japan a special position in Asia: China should accept only Japanese military or technical advisers, and no foreign loans were to be made to China without Japanese agreement. The declaration was evidently incompatible with the policy of the open door in China, and was disavowed by the Japanese government, but in November 1934 an oil monopoly law was passed in Manchukuo which no less blatantly infringed the open door principle.

It was now becoming clear that Britain's commercial interests in China would be seriously threatened if Japan's advance continued unchecked, for British trade with the new state of Manchukuo had dropped to about one-quarter of that formerly conducted with Manchuria. Two attempts were made to restore the Anglo-Japanese co-operation in the Far East that had been so rudely interrupted by the attack on Manchuria. A nongovernmental mission of the Federation of British Industries visited Japan and Manchukuo, but had little success in spite of offers to press for a recognition of Manchukuo in London. The government itself then took a hand and sent a mission to China under the leadership of Sir Frederick Leith-Ross. It seems that the idea of the mission came from the Treasury, this being one of the earliest known interventions in foreign affairs by Neville Chamberlain, then Chancellor of the Exchequer. The object of the mission was to conciliate Japan by tacitly accepting Japanese control of Manchukuo, and thence to convince her that her best interests lay in participation in international development of China's resources and trade. China would be relieved of Japanese pressure, and the spirit of the Washington nine-power treaty would be restored.

The attempt failed, partly because the Japanese were reluctant to believe that Britain genuinely intended to cut her losses and was willing to compound with aggression, and partly because they had no effective means of checking the profitable smuggling of silver conducted by their nationals in north China. Rebuffed in Tokyo, Leith-Ross turned his attention to direct negotiation with China. Here he had striking success. With his assistance the Chinese prepared a plan for reform of the currency based on the nationalization of silver and making government notes sole legal tender. Details of the reform were announced on 3 November 1935, and simultaneous proclamation in London and Hong Kong of British acceptance and support ensured its success. The effects of Japanese silver smuggling, and of the increase in the price of silver in external markets in 1934, were thus counteracted, and the Chinese economy made a startling recovery in the early months of 1936.

The refusal of Japan to co-operate with the Leith-Ross mission, and the success of the mission in China, placed Britain and Japan in open opposition in the Far East. The Japanese thesis that only she could revive China was seen to be unsound, and the Japanese expansionists realized that time was against their ambition to be masters of the east: a unified nationalist China, militarily revitalized by German officers and economically restored by British support, would be bound soon to become the dominant power in the Far East if her recovery were not checked. Japan's opportunity came in 1937. The isolationist attitude of the United States, first apparent in the Pacific in the passing of the Philippines Independence Act in 1934, was confirmed by the strengthened Neutrality Act of May 1937. Soviet unwillingness to oppose Japan had been apparent in the 1934 sale of Soviet rights in the Chinese Eastern Railway in Manchukuo, and the great purges, which shook the Soviet military and economic structure to its foundations, were moving towards their highest pitch of intensity. In Europe Italy's invasion of Abyssinia had revealed the weakness of Anglo-French policy in the League, while Nazi Germany had got away with the remilitarization of the Rhineland in defiance of Locarno: if Britain and France could not or would not act so near home, there was little likelihood that they would forcibly oppose a renewed Japanese thrust southwards. A clash between Chinese and Japanese troops on 7 July at the Marco Polo bridge near Peking was accordingly taken as a pretext for a Japanese attempt to detach the five northern provinces of China. Despite early losses the Chinese refused to accept defeat, though offered peace on Japan's terms in December. They were gradually forced away from the coast and out of Nanking, Hankow, and

Canton, but the conflict (war was never declared by Japan) came to an end only with the unconditional surrender of Japan to Britain and the United States in August 1945.

The Sino-Japanese war produced a diplomatic alignment of the powers in the Far East similar to that in Europe. Hitherto Germany and Britain had been natural allies in the Far East, both having extensive interests in China, and both being faced with the major question of whether to join with Japan against the Soviet Union with a view to joint exploitation of China, or whether to oppose the establishment of exclusive Japanese control over China, which implied a policy parallel with that of the U.S.S.R. Britain's attempt in the Leith-Ross mission at co-operation with Japan in the development of China had failed: Germany achieved alliance with Japan in the anti-Comintern pact of 25 November 1936, but secured no guarantee of co-operation with Japan in China. She retained her military advisers with Chiang Kai-shek and continued to supply him with war materials. When the Sino-Japanese war broke out, Germany was forced to choose between continued friendship with Japan, and defence of her interests in China through continued support to Chiang Kai-shek. Conflict in Berlin between Neurath and Ribbentrop on this issue ended with the appointment of the latter to the Foreign Ministry on 4 February 1938, and among the new minister's earliest actions were the recognition of Manchukuo, the cessation of arms deliveries to China, and the withdrawal of military advisers from Chiang Kai-shek. There is perhaps poetic justice in the way Japan used Germany's commitments in Europe to destroy her position and interests in China in a precisely similar manner to that employed by Germany in using Mussolini's commitments in Spain to destroy Italy's position and interests in Austria.[1]

Ribbentrop's abandonment of China and alignment of Germany with Japan left Britain alone in defence of her Far Eastern interests, although the hostility of the United States to further Japanese encroachments was steadily increasing. Britain none the less did not wholly abandon her attempt to safeguard her position in China and satisfy Japanese ambitions through appeasement: in mid-1939 the German ambassador in Moscow,

[1] See *Documents on German Foreign Policy, 1918-1945*, Series D, Volume I, Chapter IV, H.M.S.O., 1949, and Chapters 10 and 11 below.

Count von der Schulenburg, reported the widespread belief that one of the reasons for Britain's reluctance to conclude a close alliance with the Soviet Union was fear lest by so doing Japan would be finally driven into the arms of Germany.[1] Early in May Halifax assured the Japanese ambassador in London that any Anglo-Soviet alliance that might be concluded would not extend in its terms to the Far East.[2] But Japan was no more to be bought off by concessions than Germany in Europe, and the increasing pressure of Italy and Germany, together with their alignment with Japan in the Far East, made it impossible for Britain effectively to defend her Far Eastern interests or aid China in her resistance. The United States administration, moreover, was able to move only with the greatest caution: the extreme isolationism expressed in the Neutrality Acts was confirmed by popular demands for the evacuation of United States citizens from China, by the sharp reaction against Roosevelt's speech of 5 October 1937 suggesting that aggressors, like infectious diseases, should be quarantined, and by the Ludlow amendment to the Constitution which would have required a national referendum before a declaration of war could be effective, and which was defeated on 10 January 1938 only by 209 votes to 188.

Japan was therefore able to flout Britain and the United States almost with impunity. China had appealed to the League on 12 September, and on 5 October the League's Far Eastern advisory commission reported that the Japanese military effort was incommensurate with the scale of the incident and was in contradiction with the Kellogg pact and the nine-power pact. The Council seized the opportunity and invited the nine powers to consult, a decision which the Assembly confirmed on the following day while recommending members to examine ways of giving individual assistance to China. The nine powers less Japan met at Brussels on 3 November, but the pressure of European problems and the unhelpful attitude of Italy ensured that no effective action would be taken without a strong lead from the United States. This Roosevelt and Hull could not give, and on 15 November the conference resolved that there was

[1] *Nazi-Soviet Relations, 1939-1941*, pp. 8-9.
[2] Woodward, E. L. and Butler, R., *Documents on British Foreign Policy, 1919-1939*, Third Series, Vol. V, p. 482.

little hope of a settlement by conciliation and that the powers should consider their attitude to Japanese aggression. The conference adjourned *sine die* on 24 November.

China's representative at Geneva, Dr. Wellington Koo, pressed China's appeals on several occasions in 1938, but Britain succeeded in preventing the adoption of sanctionary measures which would either have ended in fiasco or would have involved her in naval commitments that she could not afford to undertake in the critical state of European affairs. None the less Anglo-Japanese relations steadily deteriorated. Britain's desire to end the conflict in the Far East by concessions to Japan did not extend to willingness to surrender financial and commercial interests valued at several hundred million pounds, or to abandon China altogether. She therefore continued to allow foreign states to export arms to China through Hong Kong, and she protested against Japanese restrictions on commerce on the Yangtze imposed, according to Japan, because of military necessity. On 11 March 1938 Japan opened a bank in Tientsin and Peking with the object of gradually converting all Chinese currency into foreign exchange, and on 13 March China retaliated by ordering the centralization of all foreign exchanges at Hankow and Hong Kong. This measure caused loss of confidence in the currency, the strength of which had already been undermined by the strains of war, and on 8 March 1939 Britain came to the rescue with a supporting loan. On 14 June matters reached a crisis with the imposition of a Japanese blockade of the British concession of Tientsin. British subjects entering or leaving the concession, including women, were seized and searched by the Japanese military, and British protests at the outrages were ignored. The pretext for the blockade the Japanese found in the sanctuary given to four Chinese suspected of terrorist activity against collaborating Chinese officials, but the methods by which it was conducted, and the magnitude of its repercussions, showed that the blockade merely marked the culmination of a steadily mounting tide of mutual hostility. The object of the Japanese army was to provoke war with Britain on an issue with which the United States might not be in full sympathy, or alternatively to force Britain to close Hong Kong to arms importation and cease her support of the Chinese economy. The Japanese government succeeded in persuading the army to allow negotiations to be transferred to Tokyo, and the major threats were averted, but the blockade was lifted only at the price of a British agreement not to interfere with measures taken by the Japanese military authorities for the purpose of maintaining law and order. By midsummer 1939, therefore, Anglo-Japanese relations had reached a point where open conflict might break out at any moment if the Japanese army pressed home its demands and if the British government refused to yield. It may well be that the open Japanese attack on Britain's Far Eastern possessions would have been launched many months before December 1941 if it had not been for the shattering effect of the Nazi-Soviet pact of August 1939 which completely destroyed the diplomatic assumptions upon which Japanese policy had been founded since 1937.

The impotence of Britain to defend her interests in the Far East, or to lead the nations assembled at Geneva to oppose open aggression according to their obligations under the League Covenant, strikingly demonstrated Britain's twentieth-century inability to defend her world-wide interests unaided. In face of the attitude of United States public opinion, the administration in Washington was unable forcibly to oppose Japanese expansion southwards, although at the end of July 1939 Cordell Hull took the effective step of denouncing the American-Japanese trade treaty of 1911. But Britain's European interests necessarily remained paramount. On 10 April "M. Bonnet again expressed great misgivings regarding our [Britain's] intention to send ships to the Far East. He said that the French Government considered this 'catastrophic'. . . . The war, if it came, would be won in Europe".[1] With this last sentiment the British government could not but agree. All the determination with which Britain had refused to commit herself to the defence of Europe was thus shown to be pointless, for the degree of freedom that she retained neither enabled her to defend her extra-European interests nor to hold herself aloof from developments in Europe. It was impossible to deny that her overseas connections with the Commonwealth and with the United States were vital to her diplomatic position in the world and to her economic health, but it remained true that her existence as an independent

[1] Woodward, E. L. and Butler, R., *Documents on British Foreign Policy, 1919-1939*, Third Series, Vol. V, p. 160.

power could be brought to an end by any state that dominated the continent of Europe. That lesson had been learned by Queen Elizabeth, and Pitt, and Grey, but its logical consequences in the changed world of the twentieth century were not appreciated by the statesmen who governed Britain in her weakened condition after the First World War.

Chapter 8

THE FIRST YEARS OF NAZI GERMANY

WHEN ADOLF HITLER became Chancellor of the German Reich on 30 January 1933 as a result of the intrigues of von Papen, the senile fears and prejudices of Hindenburg, and the weakness of the Social Democrats and von Schleicher, few people outside Germany had read *Mein Kampf*. Of those in Britain who had read it, the majority could not believe that its author had every intention of carrying out its programme when he gained power. The full horror of Nazism was only implicit in the philosophy and behaviour of its exponents before power was won, and the ultimate depths of its evil were such as to be all but incredible. Penetrating and instructive as the dispatches of the British ambassador in Berlin, Sir Horace Rumbold, were, his prescience was not, and could not reasonably be expected to have been, sufficient to warn his government of the true measure of the dangers now confronting them. The members of the government in London can hardly be blamed at this early date for failing to base their policy towards the new Germany on an assessment of the nature of Nazism which later events were abundantly to justify, but which in 1933 was founded on scrappy and inconclusive evidence.

The decisive error of the Kaiser in Hitler's view had been to get himself involved in war with Britain as well as with France and Russia. In *Mein Kampf* Hitler therefore declared his aim to be alliance with Britain and with the other power he considered dynamic, Italy. In the early 'thirties the circumstances were propitious for the achievement of this aim. British impatience with the apparent intransigence of France over reparations and disarmament had been greatly increased by the World Economic Crisis, and particularly in the Labour party pacifism combined with concern for the standard of living to make the cause of disarmament ever more alluring. Irritation with France not unnaturally produced growing sympathy with Germany, and thus paradoxically enough the political groups in Britain that

99

might have been expected to feel greater concern for the fate of the working-class parties in Germany were in these early years even more in favour of accommodation with Germany than the predominantly Conservative government. The situation in the Far East, secondly, remained critical. Relations with the Soviet Union, in the third place, were in 1933 again strained by the arrest of certain British subjects employed by Metropolitan-Vickers Limited in Moscow; and in the same year the isolationist attitude of the new Roosevelt administration in the United States was demonstrated at the World Economic Conference when the President decided, for internal financial reasons, to lower the value of the dollar, apparently regardless of the effect of the decision on international economic relations. While, therefore, such danger-signals as the greatly expanded financial provision for armaments in the German budget of March 1934 could not be ignored, none the less the British government was eager to seize any chance of satisfying Germany's legitimate claims in a general settlement that would lower the temperature in Europe, and British government and opposition alike condemned the French reaction to Germany's budgetary announcement of rearmament.[1]

The climate was hardly favourable for discussions in 1934 with the internal struggle in Germany leading to the Roehm purge on 30 June, and the attempted seizure of Austria in the Dollfuss *Putsch* on 25 July. The British opportunity came, however, with Hitler's announcement on 15 January 1935 that he had no further territorial claims on France now that the plebiscite in the Saar had shown a heavy majority in favour of returning to Germany. Anglo-French discussions which swiftly followed this announcement by Hitler ended in the publication of a communiqué on 3 February. The communiqué reverted to the formula of December 1932 by which Germany had been persuaded back into the World Disarmament Conference—"equality of rights in a system which would provide security for all nations"—proposed a German re-entry into the League, the supersession of Part V of the Versailles treaty which dealt with German disarmament, and German participation in a security agreement covering the countries of eastern Europe and in a

[1] See Chapter 2, p. 33.

mutual assistance pact modelled on Locarno which should operate in the case of unprovoked aerial aggression by one of the contracting parties upon another. Pursuant to their aim of gaining British friendship and thus isolating France, the Nazis swiftly responded by inviting the British Foreign Secretary, Sir John Simon, and the Lord Privy Seal, Mr. Anthony Eden, to visit Berlin. Arrangements were made for the visit to take place early in March. The timing was, however, hardly fortunate, for a government review of Britain's defence position which had recently been completed had led to the conclusion that some British rearmament was necessary. This conclusion was published in a white paper on 4 March explaining the reasons for the decision, chief among which was the fact that Germany and other nations were themselves rearming.

The attitude of the Liberal and official Labour oppositions to rearmament was made abundantly clear by Sir Herbert Samuel and Mr. Attlee in a debate on 11 March, when they suggested that publication of the white paper was tactless and ill-timed in view of the German invitation, and necessary, if at all, only because of the government's sabotage of collective security. Baldwin himself for the government was defensive and almost apologetic in tone. But Hitler, with his unrivalled flair for recognizing and exploiting opportunities, developed a diplomatic cold and brought about the postponement of the Simon/Eden visit. On 9 March Goering announced that a German air force was in existence, and a week later on the 16th, after the mild reaction to this first open repudiation of a clause of the Versailles treaty had been noted, a decree was promulgated in Germany re-introducing conscription. The pretext for this decree was the debate in the French Chamber on the government's decision to double the length of service of French conscripts in order to prevent the fall in recruits that would otherwise have resulted from the low birth-rate in France between the years 1915 and 1919, but the German army of five hundred and fifty thousand men envisaged by the decree was far higher than the normal French peace-time strength, and the decree itself, like the announcement about the air force, was a flat repudiation of the disarmament clauses of the Versailles treaty.

The consistent French opposition to German parity in armaments, at least until an inspection system was effectively working, had been undermined by the reference in the 3 February communiqué to abrogation, under certain conditions, of Part V of the Versailles treaty; but she naturally joined with Italy, still mindful of the Dollfuss *Putsch* of the previous July, in an official protest against this unilateral denunciation of Versailles. In London, however, Sir John Simon had announced in the House of Commons four days after the German air force announcement that his postponed visit to Berlin was now arranged for 25 March, and after the promulgation of the conscription decree the British government's reaction was to enquire whether the German government still considered the visit desirable. The Germans were only too happy to widen the opening breach between Britain and France.

In these circumstances no effective action could emerge from the meeting of the three former Allies at Stresa between 11 and 14 April, or from the meeting of the League Council on 17 April. A communiqué issued from Stresa on 14 April suggested a new unity among Britain, France and Italy, a unity swiftly to be known as the Stresa Front. The three powers agreed on the policy of safeguarding Austria's independence, they registered their opposition to changes in the *status quo* in Europe, and they denounced the unilateral abrogation of the military clauses of Versailles. The League Council's resolution on 17 April echoed these last two conclusions. It appears that the French made no attempt to go beyond a formal protest either at Stresa or at Geneva:[1] such an attempt would clearly have failed had the French desired to make it in view of the fact that the Simon/Eden visit to Berlin had taken place as planned.

Within five months the Stresa Front was in ruins. During the visit of the British ministers to Berlin, the Nazis had shown themselves unwilling to consider an eastern security pact as proposed in the Anglo-French communiqué, or to return to the League without some satisfaction of their colonial claims, but they had made a skilful play for British goodwill by affirming that the German navy would not be allowed to exceed thirty-five per cent of the British. In order to compensate for the failure of the proposal for an eastern pact, and to counter the evidently increasing power of Germany, France on 2 May initialled, not without misgivings, a mutual assistance pact with the Soviet Union and

[1] François-Poncet, A., *Souvenirs d'une Ambassade à Berlin*, pp. 232-4.

thus entered into an association that Britain viewed with caution if not open distrust. On 18 June a naval agreement between Britain and Germany was signed by which Germany agreed to limit her fleet to thirty-five per cent of the British fleet, with the exception of submarines which she could build up to parity with the whole Commonwealth subject to notification of exceeding forty-five per cent of the total of Commonwealth submarines. In October Mussolini launched his long-planned offensive against Abyssinia, and Britain took the lead in organizing sanctions under the League of Nations Covenant against him.

Thus by the beginning of the third year of Nazi power the pattern of international relationships of the 1920s had been fundamentally altered. The Soviet Union had emerged from isolation, had entered the League of Nations and had initialled a mutual assistance agreement with France, the most rigid defender of the *status quo* in Europe. Italy had launched an aggressive attack in East Africa and had thereby incurred the opposition of Britain within the League: the former cordiality of Anglo-Italian relations had been irretrievably shattered. France, fearful of the new might of Germany, unable to obtain any assurances about German intentions towards her east European allies, rightly uncertain of the degree of support that she could command for her policies in London, had reluctantly turned to alliance with the Communist power in the east. Britain—impatient with the seeming intransigence of France towards Germany, distrustful of the new French association with a power with which Britain's relations had been strained when not formally ruptured, hostile under the pressure of public opinion to Italy's open violation of the Covenant in Ethiopia, alive to, while not fully comprehending the nature of, the Nazi menace—Britain felt no unalloyed sympathy with any of the continental powers. Government and Opposition thought alike on this, however much they may have differed on methods and immediate policies. The Anglo-German naval agreement was symptomatic of this outlook, for while it reduced, at least on paper, the possibility of danger from the Nazis to this country, it sharply repudiated any idea that might have existed in French or Italian minds that the Stresa agreement implied any general association of Britain with French policies.

The naval agreement not unnaturally produced vigorous protest from Paris, for it involved British acceptance of a modification of the disarmament clauses of Versailles, the unilateral denunciation of which by Germany had been condemned by all three powers at Stresa. The British replied to this protest with the argument of expediency that it was better to get Germany voluntarily to limit herself to a reasonable level of armaments than to adopt a high moral attitude towards treaty violation, to refuse to discuss the matter, and thus in effect to acquiesce in unlimited German rearmament. This somewhat specious argument ignored the fact that it was Germany's object to isolate France by gaining Britain's good will. The expression of this policy in the field of armaments was the planning of land forces far in excess of those France normally maintained, but restriction of naval forces to a level well below that of the British fleet. But in Britain impatience with France and consequent sympathy with Germany had now reached a point where the British saw themselves no longer as the ally of a wronged country against an aggressor but as the mediator between two parties to a dispute in which faults were to be found on both sides.

This attitude was soon to receive striking confirmation in a far more serious crisis, the German remilitarization of the Rhineland. On 21 May 1935 Hitler had made one of his most important policy speeches in the Reichstag. In the course of the speech he referred somewhat obscurely to the effects of the Franco-Soviet pact on German relations with France, but asserted that he was concerned to repudiate only the discriminatory clauses of Versailles, and that he would maintain voluntarily signed treaties. Of these Locarno was presumably one, and in October the British ambassador, Sir Eric Phipps, was in fact informed by the German Foreign Minister that the German government agreed that all provisions of the treaty of Locarno—which reaffirmed the demilitarization of the Rhineland—continued to be in force.[1] On 27 February 1936 a vote was at last taken in the French Chamber on ratification of the

---

[1] Comd. 5143, 1936. *Correspondence showing the course of certain Diplomatic Discussions directed towards securing An European Settlement, June 1934 to March 1936*, p. 58.

Franco-Soviet pact, and two weeks later a similar and also favourable vote was taken in the Senate. On 28 February Hitler said in an interview with a French journalist that he wanted peace with France, and during a talk with Hitler on 2 March the French ambassador, M. François-Poncet, asked for proposals to this end, which Hitler promised to prepare. The next news received in the capitals of Europe was a circular from Berlin on 7 March saying that the Franco-Soviet pact was directed against Germany and had destroyed the basis of Locarno, so German troops were marching into the demilitarized zone of the Rhineland. Using the technique which was later to become familiar, Hitler attached to this announcement of violation both of a treaty and of his pledged word a memorandum containing attractive-looking proposals for a twenty-five year Franco-Belgian-German non-aggression pact with British and Italian guarantees, an air pact, non-aggression pacts with states of eastern Europe, and a German re-entry into the League if the Covenant were separated from the Versailles treaty and the question of colonies were examined in a sympathetic spirit.

The German remilitarization of the Rhineland is recognized now as the turning-point in Hitler's career of aggression. It was the last occasion upon which the Nazis could certainly have been stopped almost without bloodshed, for only a few battalions were sent into the Rhineland, and these against the wishes of the German General Staff and with orders to withdraw if the French marched. The Rhine frontier was rapidly fortified by Germany, thereby greatly increasing the hazards of any French action in support of her eastern allies if they should be threatened. Whatever the reasons for the failure of France to act against this direct threat to her security, her prestige was undermined throughout Europe, and the confidence of her allies was diminished. Evidence of this was soon to be found in the fall of the pro-French Rumanian Foreign Minister Titulescu in August, and in Leopold of Belgium's proclamation in October of his renunciation of the French alliance and reversion to Belgium's 1839 status of neutrality.

The French were not unaware of these likely consequences of the German action, and the Cabinet apparently considered immediate mobilization. At length it was decided to notify the League Council of the violation of Locarno and call the Locarno guarantors into conference. Among the reasons for rejecting immediate military action and adopting this procedure was undoubtedly the preference of London for this course, and the reluctance of the French government to provoke an open breach with Britain and thus grant Hitler one of his objects.[1] For opinion in London was all but unanimous. In addition to the general measure of sympathy felt with German grievances, it was considered that Germany had some ground for objecting to the encirclement implied by the Franco-Soviet pact. The contrast was widely drawn between the Italian aggression against an independent state-member of the League (effective League action in aid of whom had been consistently hampered by the French[2]), and the German action which merely consisted in marching troops into German territory. *The Times* leader on 9 March was headed "A Chance to Rebuild". On the same day Baldwin in the House of Commons, while guaranteeing France and Belgium against a German attack, affirmed his conception of Britain not merely as a guarantor but also as a mediator by saying: "In Europe we have no more desire than to keep calm, to keep our heads and to continue to try to bring France and Germany together in a friendship with ourselves."[3]

It was clear, then, that Britain, while still keeping to her Locarno commitment to defend France and Belgium against attack, was by no means prepared to countenance a military reaction to the German move, whether conducted by the French in isolation or under the auspices of the Locarno powers. Italy, hitherto firm against Nazi expansion, saw in the Rhineland remilitarization a means of gaining British and French acquiescence to her African conquests. Belgium, desirous of retaining her good relations with London, and already losing confidence in France's ability to defend her, was reluctant to support the French in advocating extreme action. When the Locarno powers met, therefore, the French Foreign Minister, Flandin, had no chance of gaining their support for sanctions against Germany; and it may well be that he was glad to use the excuse of British opposi-

---

[1] Flandin, P.-E., *Politique française 1919-1940*, pp. 198-202. Paris, Editions Nouvelles, 1947.

[2] See Chapter 9, *passim*.

[3] *Parly. Debs.*, Fifth Series, H. of C., Vol. 309, col. 1841.

tion as a way of avoiding the responsibility of decisions which might have brought about the fall of his government, and the ultimate consequences of which could not be foreseen. At length the four powers reached an agreement which was initialled on 19 March. The French demand that Germany should not be allowed to fortify the new frontier was accepted. Britain, France and Belgium agreed to open staff talks on joint defence plans—this representing a tightening of Britain's commitment to France in the form that Curzon had firmly rejected in 1922. It was proposed that the matter should be submitted to arbitration at the Hague—a proposal that Germany had already rejected by claiming the issue to be political and not legal in nature. Finally the four powers suggested that an international police force should be sent to occupy a narrow zone on the frontier, this suggestion being made by Britain to gain time and give the French an excuse for holding back. The justification of the last proposals, as Eden said in the House, was "that at a moment of crisis they allayed the immediate prospects of steps being taken which might have led to war. They earned us a breathing space. . . ."[1] The proposals, together with the demand that the new frontier should not be fortified, were rejected by Germany in a preliminary reply on 24 March: a definitive memorandum on 31 March did not again refer to either the proposals or the demand. Eden insisted at a further meeting of the Locarno powers on 10 April that negotiations could not be said to have broken down, and he induced France to agree to his sending a questionnaire to Berlin asking for elucidation of certain points in the memorandum. On 2 May the Sarraut/Flandin government was defeated at the polls, the new Popular Front government under the pacifist Léon Blum was not formed until 4 June, Eden's elucidatory questionnaire was never answered by Germany, and during a visit to London on 23 July Blum agreed to join Britain in an attempt to construct a new Locarno-type system. He thus tacitly accepted the *fait accompli* of 7 March.

However thankful Flandin may have been at being able to cast the blame for French inaction on British shoulders, it is clear that in this first decisive crisis in Germany's career of aggression, British policy had played a crucial part. Apart from the Communists and a few isolated leaders of opinion, the great

[1] *Parly. Debs.*, Fifth Series, H. of C., Vol. 310, cols. 1445-6.

majority of the people of Britain supported the government's policy. The official opposition indeed considered that the government had gone too far in meeting French desires: in the debate in the House of Commons on 26 March Dalton and Attlee attacked the international police force idea, because it would mean including Italians, attacked any idea of sanctionary measures against Germany, and denounced the guarantee to France and still more the military alliance implied in the agreement to open staff talks. It is a striking commentary upon the distance travelled by the opposition between 1936 and 1938 that in the former year the government was denounced for giving a guarantee to France, while in the latter year Chamberlain was no less vigorously condemned for refusing to give an unequivocal guarantee to France in case she should be involved in war with Germany on account of her obligations to Czechoslovakia. Had understanding of the real nature of Nazism been more exact, had the government been less desirous of making a general and lasting agreement with Germany and holding the balance in Europe, had the opposition and a large part of public opinion been less incensed with France because of her consistent rigidity of policy against Germany now capped by her sabotaging of the cause of collective security through obstructing the development of sanctions against Italy, Hitler would never have been allowed to get away with this second and more striking triumph. But it was to take three more, and greater, blows before the country was to be united in its realization that Nazism had to be destroyed.

Chapter 9

THE ABYSSINIAN CRISIS

IT MAY BE doubted whether even Hitler would have risked sending his troops into the Rhineland had not the opportunity been created for him by the Italian attack on Abyssinia. Mussolini's decision to attempt the conquest of Abyssinia had been taken in the autumn of 1933.[1] There is little point in trying to construct a logical explanation of any action of the Italian dictator, prey as he was to impulse and the influence of emotion, unreasonably sensitive to the figure he cut by his public actions, and subject to long periods of indecision and vacillation between the course that prudence and the interests of his country demanded, and the course dictated by the needs of his own ego. Nevertheless it is possible to discern some of the influences that led to this aggressive attack, which was of crucial importance for the fate of the world in the 1930s. Little versed as Mussolini was in economics, he yet could appreciate both the economic and political effects of the World Economic Crisis in Italy, and he needed to act in some way that would restore the confidence of the Italian people in his leadership. Ever since coming to power in 1922 his speeches had constantly extolled the virtues of force, and gradually and more clearly he had unfolded the theme of a new Roman Empire in which the Mediterranean would be an Italian sea. At the same time Mussolini, like all politically minded Italians, was well aware that the greatest benefit Italy had derived from the First World War was control of the northern frontier and the Brenner Pass, on the other side of which now lay not the mighty Austro-Hungarian Empire, but the small and weak Republic of Austria. Mussolini may well have hoped that the conquest of Abyssinia would secure his East African colonies of Eritrea and Somaliland from any danger of attack if he were involved in a European conflict. It might also strengthen Italy's economic position, so that he could more confidently defend Austrian

[1] de Bono, E., *Anno XIIII*, p. 13. The Cresset Press, 1937.

independence and pursue more vigorously his exploitation of Balkan dissensions, his intrigues in North Africa, and his long-term aspiration of turning the Mediterranean into *mare nostrum*. Control of Abyssinia itself could directly serve that aim, since it would in some degree neutralize Aden and thus threaten freedom of passage through the Suez Canal. The enterprise did not appear to be fraught with any great danger since the League would not act without British and French leadership: France in 1933 was clearly becoming more and more concerned with the problem of security against Germany, and Britain's weakness or complacency towards adventures of this kind had apparently been amply demonstrated in the Manchurian crisis.

Mussolini's calculations about France were fully justified in the event. The collapse of the World Disarmament Conference, the open German avowal of rearmament in the March 1934 budget, the signature of the Polish-German non-aggression pact of January 1934, the failure of Barthou either to weld more tightly the relations of the smaller east European states with each other and with France, or to construct an eastern Locarno, the Nazi attempt in Austria in July 1934, and the whole tone and philosophy of Nazism—all these led French statesmen desperately to seek new and firm alliances with which to confront the mounting German power. In January 1935 the French Prime Minister Laval visited Rome and settled in a manner largely favourable to France the chief questions in dispute between the two countries in Tunisia and East Africa, and in addition reached agreement with Mussolini on the policy the two countries should adopt towards Germany and Austria. What else passed between the two men is unknown, and the evidence from Flandin, from the later Italian Foreign Minister, Ciano, from the French Commander-in-Chief, Gamelin, and from Laval himself, is conflicting. Certainly in exchange for this highly satisfactory agreement from the French point of view Laval offered Mussolini an economic free hand in Abyssinia: what political concessions he made, if any, and whether he promised to turn a blind eye to the coming Italian aggression, cannot be determined in the light of available information. But at the very least Mussolini's opinion that France would do all she could to avoid interference was emphatically confirmed, if he did not receive formal assurances that France would take no action.

Mussolini's only likely opponent then was Britain. In this case too the omens were not wholly inauspicious. Not merely had previous violations of treaties and of the Covenant by Germany and Japan passed without effective response, but at the Stresa conference in April, called to deal with German conscription, Britain had joined with France and Italy in agreeing to maintain the *status quo* in *Europe*. Moreover, the question of Abyssinia was not raised at Stresa,[1] although the impending Italian aggression was now clearly evidenced by the men and war materials and supplies that had been pouring into Eritrea and Italian Somaliland for the previous few months. It looked as if Britain too would pass by on the far side, an impression that was to be strengthened in the next few months.

What, then, were the elements of British policy in this crisis? They are harder to determine in this issue than in any other major problem in the inter-war years, because the documentation at this date [1953] is less complete than for any other important question. There can be little doubt that the government's attention had been drawn to the implications for the British Empire of Mussolini's desire to establish Italian predominance in the Mediterranean. The Mediterranean had for Britain an importance economic, strategic and diplomatic. Economically, Britain had large capital investments in Greece, Turkey, Palestine, but above all Egypt, and the inland sea was an essential link in Britain's trade routes with the east; strategically, control of the Suez area and freedom of passage through the Mediterranean might be decisive for the survival of the Empire in war; diplomatically, Britain's world influence in part depended on her ability to assist small maritime powers like Greece and Turkey or powers with overseas interests such as Portugal. An Italian conquest of Abyssinia, while presenting no very great immediate danger, nevertheless carried a latent threat, and was at least ominous as a symptom of Italian desires to pass from words to deeds.

In the second place, and possibly of decisive importance in stirring the government to action in defence of imperial interests, was the influence of public opinion. It is unusual to accord such a high place to the influence of popular opinion on foreign policy, but in this case special forces were at work. The League

[1] *Parly. Debs.*, Fifth Series, H. of C., Vol. 304, col. 2934.

of Nations Union had reached the height of its activity and powers in the organization of the so-called Peace Ballot on 27 January 1935 when a crushing majority of votes in a heavy poll was cast in favour of economic sanctions against an aggressor, and a still large though less overwhelming majority favoured military sanctions also. The League of Nations idea now clearly carried enormous appeal, and the maintenance of peace tied in with the Labour opposition's advocacy of disarmament. Indications such as these could not be ignored by any government, still less by a government well into the fourth year of its existence and therefore necessarily soon to come before the electorate.

On the other hand, contrary influences worked in the opposite direction. Ardently though public opinion supported the League, there was an evident widespread failure in the public mind to understand the implications of collective security—that collective security, if enforced against an aggressor, meant war, and that meant armaments. This widespread illusion that the League was a universal and painless solvent of all problems was fostered by the title of the Peace Ballot, and may be traced to the failure of the government to point an unpopular lesson, and to the Labour opposition's policy of refusing to countenance rearmament in support of any but a collective security policy, so that (given their view that the government did not believe in collective security) they appeared at one and the same time as champions of the League and opponents of rearmament. The government in determining its policy towards Italy, however, could not but take into account both the considerable measure of disarmament that had been undertaken in Britain, and the widespread hostility to any idea of war in large sections of the British electorate. This is not to say that had the issues been made clear they would not have been faced—certain indications suggest that they might have been—but it would have taken bold and courageous leadership, confident in the correctness of its policy, to have stressed after a general election had been fixed for 14 November that the sanctions policy adopted by the government after the Italian attack in October might mean war.

Three other factors the government had to take into account. One was the evident reluctance of France under Laval to go along with a policy of stopping Italy; and however impatient were wide sections of British opinion at the French attitude to disarmament and the German problem, it would clearly be hazardous in the extreme to attempt to organize the League against Italy without the firm support of France. In the second place, the attitude of the United States was non-committal: the first Neutrality Acts, passed in May 1935, empowered the President to impose an embargo on the shipment of arms to belligerents, but gave him no discretion to place an embargo on shipments to one side only in a conflict, and did not apply to materials needed in war; so that there was no guarantee that if economic sanctions were imposed by the League on an aggressive Italy, their effect would not largely be vitiated by greatly expanded exports from America. Finally, Britain, though not to the same extent as France, was becoming concerned about the revival of German power and the attitude of the Nazi government, and at least one powerful adviser in the person of Sir Robert Vansittart, then Permanent Under-Secretary of State for Foreign Affairs, was loath to alienate Italy and thus lose her from the anti-Nazi camp.

Amidst these conflicting influences—the possible latent threat to the Empire, the real threat to Geneva, popular faith in the League system, the absence of readiness for war, the coolness of France, the aloofness of the United States, the menace of Germany—the government's policy moved tortuously and hesitantly. An initial policy of firmness was followed by an attempt to buy the Italian dictator off, this in turn being followed by a policy of bluff coupled with limited action. The first serious indication that an Italo-Abyssinian conflict might be imminent came in December 1934 when an armed clash occurred between Italian and Abyssinian troops near a settlement named Walwal in an area where the frontier between Abyssinia and Italian Somaliland had never been precisely defined. On 3 January 1935 Abyssinia appealed to the League to settle the dispute by "wise and effectual" action under Article 11, but the appeal was not immediately heard. On 17 March, with the mounting evidence of impending Italian aggression, Abyssinia appealed under Article 15, the article empowering the Council to report on a dispute and to make recommendations which, if unfavourable to one of the parties, required the automatic application of sanctions under Article 16. The Italian ambassador in London, Count Dino Grandi, is reported to have twice tried, in January and May, to open conversations with Britain in order that the imperial interests of the two powers could be delimited, but Sir John Simon apparently replied that those interests had been determined by the Anglo-Franco-Italian agreement of 1925, and that anyway Britain could not negotiate in an atmosphere of impending aggression.

But it was soon evident that Mussolini was not to be stopped this way. The big shipments of war material and men continued, and in May Mussolini wrote in a letter to de Bono: "There has even been talk of taking 'steps'. . . . I have made it understood that we shall not turn back at any price."[1] Britain now exerted herself in earnest to prevent the conflict breaking out, for only so could she avoid having to decide among the conflicting influences on her policy. She joined with a willing France in getting consideration of the issue at Geneva postponed, and when Italy at length appointed arbitrators under the Italo-Abyssinian treaty of 1928 Britain and France again persuaded the Council on 25 May to defer consideration of the dispute until the outcome of the arbitration was known. Taking advantage of the breathing-space thus obtained Anthony Eden, newly appointed Minister for League of Nations Affairs, was sent to Rome on 24 June to attempt to buy Mussolini off. Eden suggested that Abyssinia should be required to cede the Ogaden area to Eritrea, and in compensation Britain would cede to Abyssinia the port of Zeila in British Somaliland. Mussolini may well not have liked the idea of Abyssinia gaining access to the sea, and he not merely rejected the proposals as insufficient, but remained wholly truculent in manner. According to Sir Samuel Hoare, Mussolini said during the discussions that "in any settlement without war he would require to annex all those parts of Abyssinia which did not form part of Abyssinia proper . . . and to control Abyssinia proper. . . . Moreover, Signor Mussolini made it also clear that if he had to go to war to secure his ends his aim would be to wipe out the name of Abyssinia from the map."[1]

Despite this unpromising discussion, Britain made one more

---

[1] de Bono, E., *Anno XIII*, p. 161.
[2] *Parly. Debs.*, Fifth Series, H. of C., Vol. 307, col. 2012.

attempt, this time in conjunction with France, to settle the issue at a conference of the three powers in Paris between 15 and 18 August. Mussolini's representative, Aloisi, rejected the Anglo-French proposals even as a basis for discussion. In the meantime the process of arbitration had broken down on 31 July through disagreement on the scope of the arbitration, and it was now perfectly apparent that Mussolini would be statisfied only with major annexations of Abyssinian territory and that he would conquer them by force if he failed to obtain them peacefully. It is also likely that he did not believe Britain or the League would intervene. In these circumstances the British government could not remain inactive in view of the rising tide of British public opinion. The attempt to settle the issue out of court had failed. The only possible course was to try to frighten Mussolini into the realization that the League might indeed move if he attacked. The danger of this course was that Britain might be forced to choose between ignominious retreat (with disastrous effects on the domestic position of the government, on Britain's international prestige, and on the authority of the League itself), and going forward with sanctions and the possibility of war, dragging with her an unwilling France, lacking the support of the United States, and helplessly watching Germany playing the lucrative part of *tertius gaudens*.

In order as far as possible to minimize this danger, and to gain French support if sanctions had to be imposed, Sir Samuel Hoare, now Foreign Secretary, met Laval on 10 September. The Cabinet had already decided that Mussolini should be publicly warned by a speech from Hoare at Geneva in which the allegiance of the British government to the cause of collective security should be proclaimed. No certain account exists of the discussions at the meeting of Hoare and Laval, but it seems likely that they agreed that military sanctions and a naval blockade should be ruled out, and that the Suez Canal should not be closed. Laval later claimed that they agreed to do nothing that might lead to war, but Hoare gave a very different angle on the discussions when he said that financial and commercial sanctions had been agreed as a first step. Without documentary evidence of this discussion and its background it is impossible to say whether Hoare's speech at Geneva the next day was bluff, or was an honest statement of British intentions which in the event were not carried out because of the government's weakness and the recalcitrance of France. Be that as it may, in this speech Hoare announced Britain's firm recognition of her obligations under the Covenant. "His Majesty's Government and the British people maintain their support of the League and its ideals as the most effective way of ensuring peace . . . the League stands, and my country stands with it, for the collective maintenance of the Covenant in its entirety, and particularly for steady and collective resistance to all acts of unprovoked aggression . . . this is no variable and unreliable sentiment, but a principle of international conduct to which they [the British nation] and their Government hold with firm, enduring and universal persistence."[1] Towards the end of the speech Hoare emphasized that Britain could not carry the burden alone ("If the burden is to be borne, it must be borne collectively. If risks for peace are to be run they must be run by all. The security of the many cannot be ensured solely by the efforts of a few, however powerful they may be."); but the dominant impression left by the speech was that if Italy attacked Abyssinia, Britain would stand by the cause of collective security within the League.

There could now be no patent withdrawal. Accordingly, five days after the Italian attack on 3 October, the League Council under British leadership declared Italy to be at war in violation of the Covenant, and proposed for the consideration of League members an arms embargo, financial sanctions, the cessation of all imports from Italy, the banning of some exports to Italy (oil not being among those listed), and measures for mutual assistance among the powers imposing sanctions. On 11 October the Assembly confirmed the Council's resolution. At the British general election on 14 November, during the campaign for which the government had pledged its support to collective security, the government was returned with a reduced but still large majority. On 18 November the sanctions proposed by the League Council on 7 October were put into effect by a vote of the League Assembly.

The results of this action were much as some British advisers had feared. Mussolini, almost certainly surprised by the League's action, complained bitterly of the contrast between his case and those of Japan in Manchuria, of the Chaco war in South America, and of Germany's violations of Versailles. He vowed

[1] League of Nations *Official Journal*, Spec. Sup. No. 138, XVI Ass. pp. 43-6.

that if oil sanctions were imposed it would mean war, and the members of the British government could not have known, however much they may have suspected, that his bellicosity in public was but a cloak for the fact that in private he was badly frightened. There was widespread support among the small powers and from the Soviet Union for collective action, but none of these could bring much assistance to Britain if Italy should declare war, although agreements were concluded with Greece, Turkey and Yugoslavia. Britain thus feared that she might find herself carrying single-handed the burden of war with Italy: she was, as Hoare was later to point out, the only member of the League to move a ship or a plane or a man. An agreement was indeed also concluded with France, the only power capable of rendering swift and powerful assistance, but Laval and later Flandin, desirous of not finally alienating their newly won Italian ally against Germany, maintained steady resistance to the imposition of the one swiftly effective economic sanction, an embargo on oil exports. Awareness of the need to keep Italy in the anti-German front was present in London also, and the foregoing considerations, together with the promptings of Vansittart, led to the initialling of the notorious Hoare-Laval plan on 8 December. The plan proposed that part of Abyssinia was to be ceded to Italy, and it is by no means certain that Mussolini would not have thankfully agreed, but the terms of the plan were allowed to leak out in Paris and they were greeted with a storm of public indignation in Britain. A helpless victim was to be sacrificed to an avowed aggressor, the League was to be thrown over, and the government's electoral promises were to be flagrantly violated. Doubtless the government would have fallen had not Winston Churchill stayed painting in Barcelona,[1] and had not the Prime Minister, Baldwin, with one of those political about-turns that so remarkably did not cause him to lose his sobriquet of "Honest Stan", repudiated his Foreign Minister's signature, which the Cabinet had approved, and appointed Eden to succeed Hoare at the Foreign Office when the latter inevitably resigned.

It being now apparent that the British government was frightened, but that no compromise settlement was possible, Mussolini finally burnt his boats by appointing Marshal Badoglio to command in East Africa and ordering him to use

---

[1] Churchill, W. S., *The Gathering Storm*, pp. 144-5. Cassell, 1948.

mustard gas in order swiftly to break the resistance of the Abyssinian armies. Eden renewed British pressure at Geneva for the imposition of oil sanctions, but the French continued unwilling, and the British government lacked the courage to risk a naval action with the Italians by using the fleet at Alexandria to close the Suez Canal. It seems that the new French Foreign Minister Flandin was prepared to consider oil sanctions against Italy in early March in return for military staff talks between Britain and France, but the possibility of Anglo-French co-operation, and any French thoughts of effective action against Italy, were shattered by the German remilitarization of the Rhineland on 7 March. Abyssinian resistance suddenly collapsed on 2 May, and the empire was annexed to the Italian crown on 9 May. The Labour opposition asserted that the German action of 7 March had been made possible by the British government, for failing to act effectively against Italy and so to live up to its professions of collective action against an aggressor: they equally violently objected to co-operation with France on the Rhineland issue, for France had even more flagrantly sabotaged the cause of collective security. The French retorted in their turn that it was Britain who had sabotaged the cause of collective security by destroying the Geneva Protocol in 1925 and the Paul-Boncour plan in 1932, but now that British imperial interests were threatened a new attachment to League principles had suddenly been discovered, even though action in this case would open the way in Europe to domination by the Nazis. Controversy now raged over whether or not sanctions should be abandoned, until at length Neville Chamberlain voiced the opinion of the majority of the government that "the policy of collective security in the circumstances in which it was tried has failed".[1] On 4 July the League Council recommended the removal of sanctions, and they were lifted on 15 July.

The Abyssinian crisis affords a classic illustration of a weak and timorous policy, swayed by conflicting influences, getting the worst of all worlds. As soon as it became clear that Mussolini was determined to attack Abyssinia, and that neither warnings nor concessions would deter him from his purpose, the British government was confronted with the choice of doing

---

[1] In a speech at the Nineteen-Hundred Club on 10 June. Quoted in Toynbee, A. J., *Survey of International Affairs 1935*, Vol. II, p. 463. O.U.P., 1936.

nothing, or of stopping Italy through the League and thereby incurring the very real risk of war with Italy, for all practical purposes single-handed. The first course was politically almost impossible in face of public opinion at home and the imminence of an election; it would weaken the League even more than Manchuria had done; and it would ignore a small and latent, but none the less real, threat to Britain's imperial position. The second course involved the risk of all the immediate hazards and tragedies attendant upon any war, for which the British people seemed unprepared, and the outcome of which could not be foreseen with certainty: it might also open the way to a swift re-establishment of German hegemony in Europe which Britain could welcome no more than a French hegemony. The British government made no clear-cut decision, but attempted to continue the combination of bluff and bribery that they had tried before Mussolini launched his attack. In guiding the League in the imposition of sanctions, Britain insisted only on those that would not be of immediate effect and so would not force Mussolini to choose between surrender and war. Had the British lead been determined, the opposition of France to oil sanctions or to closure of the Suez Canal could have been overborne or ignored, but such a course the government had not the courage or confidence to pursue. In the light of present knowledge it is clear that Britain could swiftly have defeated Mussolini, and might well have provoked his fall: the condemnation of British policy stems not from this but from the government's failure to follow to its necessary end the course of action upon which they themselves had decided. By their half-measures they ensured that the League was indeed weakened, and far more grievously than if they had done nothing; British public opinion was rent and divided and the great strength of the government's position was destroyed; through these divisions and through French weakness and discouragement the way was opened to Nazi mastery of Europe; and with it all, the alliance of Italy was permanently lost. Mussolini, bitter at Britain's treachery, fearful of the consequences of his action, triumphant in his victory and contemptuous of the fifty nations led by one whom he had successfully defied—Mussolini could never again be content in friendship with the west, and his eyes had now been turned towards the road that was to end in a public square in Milan.

Chapter 10

THE SPANISH CIVIL WAR

THE PROCESS BY which Mussolini was driven into Hitler's arms was begun by Abyssinia. It was completed by the Spanish Civil War. For some time Mussolini had been in touch with leaders of the Spanish right, and it seems clear that he had fore-knowledge of the attempt at a military *coup d'état* planned in the early months of 1936 by a group of Spanish general led by Sanjurjo and Franco. Arrangements were made in Rome for the despatch of military supplies to the Spanish generals, and a few Italian aircraft had reached Morocco before the attempted *coup*. Although the generals did not move until the night of 17/18 July, two days after sanctions on Italy were lifted by the League, the plans for Italian assistance had clearly been made while sanctions were still in force, and there is little doubt that the thought of seeing installed on France's southern frontier a government friendly to himself and established with his aid gave Mussolini lively satisfaction. Moreover, a nationalist-minded Spanish government, might, if suitably encouraged, revive Spain's long-standing claims to Gibraltar. This would at least seriously embarrass Britain, who had organized the League against Italy, and might also help Mussolini towards the achievement of his aim of domination of the Mediterranean. At the same time he was no doubt concerned at the possibility of the Communists gaining control of the Popular Front government elected in Spain in February, and thus all things combined to encourage his intervention. But the first shock of the League's action against him in Abyssinia was now to be followed by a no less disagreeable experience. He had anticipated a swift and almost bloodless *coup* in the tradition of the many that had previously occurred in Spanish history. But to his annoyance, and later his consternation, the *coup* did not succeed, but merely began a civil war that was to drag on until March 1939. Once Italy's assistance to the insurgents became known, Italian prestige was increasingly involved until it became impossible for Mussolini to extricate himself before Franco's victory had been won. His military resources were drained away to Spain, his relations with France and to a less extent Britain became steadily more strained, and he found himself diplomatically and in some degree militarily dependent on German support. He could not break from Germany without abandoning Spain, and he could not abandon Spain without admitting error and confessing defeat. For Mussolini anything was better than that.

A study of British foreign policy is not the place for an analysis of the causes of the Spanish Civil War. Nevertheless some consideration of its character is necessary if that policy is to be intelligible. In the inter-war period only Munich aroused more bitter disputation within Britain (and within France) than the Spanish Civil War. Supporters of the Spanish government considered the insurgents "Fascists": supporters of Franco believed the government to be "Reds". Neither description had more than the faintest substratum of truth. The Communists were only a very small minority on the government side, and though their influence rapidly increased after the autumn of 1936 because the Soviet Union alone among foreign powers allowed the government to buy arms, it as rapidly declined after 1937 when the U.S.S.R. turned from Spain to face more urgent dangers in Austria and Czechoslovakia. The only element on the rebel side that might properly be called Fascist was the Falange, and though its influence also at times increased, the army lost its ultimate ascendancy only for a brief period. The two sides were, however, deeply divided among themselves, and the choice made by each individual Spaniard (neutrality was almost impossible) depended on whether in his personal case political, economic, social or religious motives were dominant. The four main groups among the insurgents were the army, the Falange, CEDA (a Catholic political association with authoritarian leanings like that of Dollfuss in Austria or Salazar in Portugal) and the Carlists (a Catholic group who idealized monarchy and the noble hierarchies which had gradually dissolved after 1815, and who were violent and intolerant towards the industrial and cultural developments of the twentieth century). The government counted among its supporters liberal intellectuals, moderate right-wing Socialists, Marxist left-wing Socialists, Communists and Anarcho-syndicalists. The major political division in Spain was between those who believed in a strong centralized government in Castile and those who wanted a federal form of government with considerable autonomy for the maritime provinces. But this division was not reflected in the civil war for, although the insurgents were centralist, the government supporters were by no means all federalist, the powerful left-wing Socialists and the Communists being both strongly centralist in outlook. Spain was also deeply divided religiously into Catholics and anti-clericals, but again the insurgents could not be described as Catholic and the government anti-clerical, for many members of the Falange could hardly be considered Christian, while on the other side the profoundly Catholic Basques were staunch supporters of the government because they hoped for provincial autonomy from the government, and this the insurgents would never grant. There were, then, differences of object, aspiration and aim within the two sides as well as between them, and rights and wrongs were inextricably intermingled. If the issue were considered in isolation, its complexity and confusion were such that non-intervention in the conflict by other powers could well be considered the only proper course.

But other powers were not willing to see the struggle fought out by the two contestants without interference from outside. In Germany, while the Foreign Office counselled caution and non-involvement, agents of the *Auslandsorganization* soon succeeded in interesting Hitler in the ideological implications of the conflict and in the economic advantages that might be derived from a victory won by Franco with German aid. German intervention never approached that of Italy in quantity, but the German technicians, the German specialist weapons, and above all the German aircraft and pilots were certainly of not less value to the insurgents than the divisions of Italian ground forces. The initial impulses to German intervention were not strong, but Hitler swiftly realized the value of the continuing contact with Italy that their several programmes of aid to Franco involved; and at a secret conference in November 1937 with his chief advisers he was to state that Germany's main interest in Spain was to keep the war going, for at best it might lead to war between Italy and the democracies, and at worst it prevented Italy breaking away from himself. During his conversation with Hitler in September 1938 after the Munich agreement was signed, Chamberlain, searching for agreement on the Spanish problem, said that he had broached the matter with Mussolini and the latter had proved most co-operative, saying that he was tired of Spain. The British minutes of the meeting note in parenthesis: "Here Herr Hitler laughed heartily."[1] Though not originally greatly concerned, Hitler thus acquired a very real interest in the Spanish struggle.

The Soviet Union, too, could hardly stand aloof. The formation of the Popular Front coalition, which had won victory at the polls in February 1936, had represented one of the few visible successes of the new Popular Front policy which had been formally approved at the seventh congress of the Comintern in the late summer of 1935 as the correct method of fighting the Fascist danger. From Moscow's point of view the Franco rising was evidently Fascist in character, and this judgment was swiftly confirmed by the mounting evidence of German and Italian assistance to the insurgents. The Soviet Union could hardly allow a government apparently formed to combat Fascism in accordance with its precepts to go under without a fight, and in October the U.S.S.R. began sending materials, technicians and military advisers to help the Spanish government.

Finally France could not but be seriously concerned at developments south of the Pyrenees. The French government in July 1936 was also a Popular Front government, headed by the Socialist Léon Blum, and supported by the Communists, and its sympathies lay strongly with the Spanish government. Strategically France's security would be greatly lessened if she had to face a hostile neighbour on her southern frontier as well as in the east and now also in the south-east. Moreover, a hostile Spain controlling the Balearic Isles, or worse still an Italian occupation of the Balearics as a reward for aiding Franco to victory, could sever French communications with Algeria, the keystone of France's imperial power. Finally, most of the groups supporting the French government were drawn from the anti-clerical wing of French politics, and the Spanish conflict thus added a new and even more bitter element to the internal dissension within France on economic and social policies.

[1] Woodward, E. L. and Butler, R., *Documents on British Foreign Policy, 1919-1939*, Third Series, Vol. II, p. 636.

With Italy and Germany intervening from the beginning on Franco's side, with the U.S.S.R. soon joining in in support of the government, and with powerful groups in France itching to do the same, there seemed to be a very real danger that the Spanish conflict might broaden into a general European war. Avoidance of this danger was the overmastering object of British policy in the Spanish crisis. The danger necessarily existed so long as any foreign state was engaged on either side, so Britain welcomed with open arms a proposal from France on 1 August 1936 that the two countries and Italy ban the export of arms or war materials to either side in the conflict. The French Cabinet had apparently at first favoured permitting private exports to Spain, but information about Italian intervention, the danger of war if French arms were sent to the other side, and the possibility that Britain might not support France if she got involved in war as a result of meddling in Spain, caused a change of mind in Paris in favour of complete non-intervention. The proposal had everything to commend itself in London. If other states would agree, it would minimize the risk of general war. It was a policy fully in line with the British traditional view that non-intervention in the internal affairs of other states was a proper principle of international conduct. How Spain was governed was of no great importance to Britain provided it was independent of the influence of any great power. Non-intervention was abundantly justified by the confusion of the issue and the absence of a clear moral case for either side. Opinion in Britain was deeply divided about the merits of the two contestants, though not so bitterly and passionately as in France, and from every point of view the only course of action seemed to be to keep clear of the conflict and persuade others to do the same.

The French proposal that the powers should declare their policies to be complete non-interference in the Spanish struggle was therefore eagerly seized upon in London, and the British government at once became and remained the chief advocate of non-intervention. By the end of August nearly thirty countries had signed declarations that their policy was one of non-intervention, and in September a committee to supervise the working of the policy was established in London under British chairmanship. Evidence of Italian and German intervention rapidly mounted, however, and in October Maisky for the Soviet Union declared that his government could remain bound by its declaration of policy only so long as other governments adhered to theirs. The sessions of the committee were occupied by charges and counter-charges of breaches of the policy declarations, and it was soon clear that flagrant intervention would continue if the movement of men and materials into Spain were not effectively controlled. Both Spanish parties refused to have foreign observers in their ports, but in February 1937 an elaborate control scheme involving naval patrols and observers on Spain's land frontiers and on ships sailing to Spain was agreed. Methods of evading the controls were, however, easily found, and in June Germany and Italy withdrew from the naval patrol after alleged attacks by Spanish government aircraft and submarines on German vessels. The patrol scheme, the two governments argued, had broken down, and the answer to the problem was to grant belligerent rights to both contestants. This the Soviet Union naturally would not accept, for belligerent rights, including the right of blockade, would greatly favour Franco whose naval forces were much superior to those of the Spanish government. The U.S.S.R. countered the German-Italian proposal by demanding that all so-called "volunteers" should be withdrawn from Spain, and discussions in the committee reached deadlock on these two opposed suggestions. The British government bent all its efforts to resolve the deadlock, and produced a compromise plan on 14 July, but the wrangle continued for a year until the Soviet rulers decided they must cut their losses and concentrate on the German threat in eastern Europe. Agreement was finally reached on the British plan on 5 July 1938, but the plan never went into operation because of the objections of the two Spanish parties.

At the cost of some opposition and much ridicule the British government thus succeeded in using the façade of non-intervention to hide much of what was happening in Spain, and to minimize the danger of the war spreading. The same policy of turning a blind eye was pursued at Geneva when the League considered the Spanish government's four appeals. The first in November 1936 was side-tracked at the instance of Britain and France, in view of proposals then coming before the non-intervention committee in London. The second in May 1937 was met by a reaffirmation of the Council's support for the non-intervention system. The fourth in April 1938, appealing directly against the non-intervention system, had no chance of success since it was considered just four days after the signature of the Anglo-Italian agreement, to which reference is made below. Only the third, in August 1937, met a measure of favourable consideration because the interests of Britain and other neutrals were directly involved. In that month there had been a sudden outbreak of submarine attacks in all parts of the Mediterranean on merchant ships of many nations, but mainly Spanish and Soviet. The suspicion at the time, that the submarines were Italian, is now confirmed[1], and this piracy, against which the Spanish government appealed, endangered the arteries through which Britain's very life-blood flowed. On this one occasion, almost unique in history, Britain, France and the U.S.S.R. acted jointly and effectively. At a conference at Nyon in September they agreed that naval patrols should be organized in the Mediterranean, and that these should destroy submarines or aircraft observed attacking non-Spanish merchant vessels. Piracy was for the time being stopped, and Britain was sufficiently alarmed to agree to a comparatively strong resolution at Geneva in response to the Spanish appeal. The resolution had no juridical effect, however, for it was defeated in the Assembly by the votes of Albania and Portugal.

These two fields of endeavour in which Britain worked to prevent the Spanish conflict spreading—the non-intervention committee and the League—were flanked by a third. The Spanish problem was constantly being discussed in the embassies of Rome, Paris and London. In these discussions Britain endeavoured to hold back France from helping the Spanish government, to limit Italian intervention, to ensure that Italy retained no permanent influence in Spain, and to restore the friendly Anglo-Italian relations that had been ruptured by Abyssinia and sanctions. A considerable advance was made by the so-called Gentlemen's agreement of 2 January 1937, in which Italy and Britain reaffirmed their intention of maintaining the *status quo* in the Mediterranean, but the good effects of this agreement were rapidly dissipated by the continuing

[1] *Ciano's Diary, 1937-1938*, p. 7. Methuen, 1952.

wrangles in the non-intervention committee, and by the re-crudescence of Franco-Italian hostility. A renewed attempt to end the discord between Rome and London was made at the instance of Chamberlain some months after he became Prime Minister in May 1937, but the Foreign Secretary, Eden, was by now of the opinion that the Axis powers, Germany and Italy, were acting in close collusion. He therefore doubted whether a settlement with one of the two could be genuine or lasting without a settlement with the other, and the test of Mussolini's good faith that he demanded before conversations should be opened was Italian execution of their declared policy of non-intervention in Spain. Chamberlain insisted, however, on making the attempt, in the belief that settlement with Italy could lead on to a settlement with Germany, and this disagreement was one of the reasons for the resignation of Eden on 20 February 1938.[1] The conversations resulted in an agreement between Italy and Britain on 16 April 1938 which contained a reaffirmation of the Gentlemen's agreement, and regulated British and Italian interests in the Mediterranean, in East Africa, in Arabia and in the Suez Canal zone. The more important part of the agreement announced a reduction of Italian forces in Libya, and a British promise to bring to the attention of the League the recognition of Italy's conquest of Abyssinia. Italy promised to support the British compromise plan for control of non-intervention and disclaimed any intention of seeking territorial, economic or political advantages in Spain. The agreement was not to come into force until the Spanish question was settled. But the expected early victory of Franco once more failed to materialize, and eventually Britain accorded recognition of Abyssinia and brought the agreement into effect on 16 November. By that date Italy had in fact withdrawn some ten thousand of her troops from Spain, and the war was dragging painfully to its close, but German-Italian relations by then had reached such a point that, as Mussolini commented to Ciano: "the Axis remains fundamental".[2]

The two main objects of British policy in Spain were to prevent the conflict spreading into a European war (as Eden put it to the Commons on 25 June 1937, "whatever may be said about 'Peace at any price,' if the right hon. Gentleman [Lloyd

[1] See Chapter 11, pp. 132-6.   [2] *Ciano's Diary*, p. 195.

George] puts it 'Peace at almost any price,' I shall scarcely quarrel with him.")[1], and secondly to ensure that Spain remained an independent country after the civil war was over. The first object was achieved, but the price paid for peace was high. The British indifference to the Spanish government's appeals to Geneva dealt the final blows to a League of Nations already weak from the shocks of Manchuria and Abyssinia; the Soviet Union found herself in effect fighting a war in isolation against the Nazis and Fascists, and she determined never to be in that position again; internal bitterness within France, so potent an element in the collapse of 1940, was greatly intensified by the inability of the government, lacking assurance of British support, to allow the Spanish government to buy the arms it needed to drive back the German- and Italian-trained and equipped forces of Franco, augmented as they were by the legions of Italy; in Britain itself the government lost its most able and honourable member, and public morale was sapped by the hollow and dishonest sham of non-intervention; Hitler trained his technicians and experimented with his new weapons, and—of far greater importance—he secured the unwilling alliance of Mussolini, who could not break with him without abandoning Spain, and who could see no advantage in alliance with the dishonourable, degenerate and decaying democracies. Had the danger of general war that Britain so greatly feared become real, Hitler would immediately have withdrawn, and it may be doubted whether Italy could have long supported Franco alone against the superior numbers of the government forces, if they had been supplied by Britain and France as well as by the Soviet Union. But the British government did not consider the merits of the case so clear that the risks involved by this course should be run.

In theory non-intervention had everything in its favour. Its flagrant breach in fact was of permanent danger to Britain only if Italian or German control over Franco was established. This the British government did not believe would happen, partly because of the repeated assurances of Italy, partly because of the traditional xenophobia of Spaniards, and partly because they judged that Franco would have to turn to Britain and the United States for economic assistance to restore his

[1] *Parly. Debs.*, Fifth Series, H. of C., Vol. 325, col. 1614.

war-shattered country. Relying on this appreciation, the government was willing to allow Franco to win even if his victory was won only through Italian and German support: they may have hoped to nullify such risk as existed by regaining the friendship of Italy. Only some such reasoning as this can explain the speech of Foreign Secretary Halifax in the Lords on 3 November 1938 which included the passage: "It has never been true, and it is not true to-day, that the Anglo-Italian Agreement had the lever value that some think to make Italy desist from supporting General Franco and his fortunes. Signor Mussolini has always made it plain from the time of the first conversations between His Majesty's Government and the Italian Government that, for reasons known to us all . . . he was not prepared to see General Franco defeated."[1] The government's calculations about the position of Franco were not wholly erroneous, for the economic weapon played a considerable part in the fight of Britain and the United States to keep Spain non-belligerent in the early years of the war. On the other hand their measurement of Mussolini remained as mistaken as it had been in 1935. The real weakness of British policy towards Spain was inherent in Chamberlain's conception of international affairs as a succession of problems to be dealt with as they arose: the Spanish Civil War was treated in the main as an isolated issue, and its effect on the whole complex of international relationships was not accurately assessed and foreseen.

[1] *Documents on International Affairs, 1938*, Vol. I, p. 109. O.U.P., 1942.

Chapter II

AUSTRIA AND CZECHOSLOVAKIA

Fall Otto (the military plans for the *Anschluss* or union of Austria with Germany) and *Fall Grün* (the plans for the destruction of Czechoslovakia) were among the earliest operations considered by Hitler. Both were necessary to his design of establishing control over the food and raw material resources of south-east Europe and the Balkans as a prelude to mastery of Europe and the conquest of the granary of the Ukraine, and both were inspired by Hitler's pan-German nationalism. As a German Austrian he burned to unite Austria with Germany, and he bitterly hated the Czechs who before 1914 had rivalled the pre-eminence of Germans in the Austrian part of the Austro-Hungarian Empire. At the secret conference in November 1937 already referred to he stated his opinion that action might be possible in 1938 if the political circumstances were sufficiently favourable.

The key importance of these two countries in barring German expansionism had long been recognized by France. "*L'Anschluss, c'est la guerre*" had been a fundamental tenet of French policy since Versailles, and in 1931 France had exerted pressure against the proposal for an Austro-German Customs Union lest political consequences should follow. French relations with Czechoslovakia had been consistently close since the country was created in 1919, and among the agreements concluded at Locarno in 1925 was a mutual assistance treaty which bound each country to come to the aid of the other if it were the victim of unprovoked aggression. Italy too had a prime interest in preventing the establishment of German control over Austria, for control of Austria meant not merely control of the Brenner Pass, but removal of a barrier to German expansion towards the Balkans and the Adriatic where Italian interests were deeply involved. Mussolini had shown his determination to defend Austrian independence when he had moved two divisions to the

Brenner in 1934 at the time of the Dollfuss *Putsch*. He grew steadily less firm in his discussions of the problem with Nazi leaders through 1936 and 1937, impelled as he was towards the Nazis by Abyssinia and dependent upon them in Spain, but he showed his continuing concern for his Balkan position by concluding a treaty with Yugoslavia in March 1937 and so ending his long feud with that country.

The attitude of Britain was much more equivocal. The European importance of the two countries was less widely recognized, the Prime Minister himself looking upon the German-Czech dispute as "a quarrel in a far-away country between people of whom we know nothing".[1] Widespread sympathy with Germany and distrust of France persisted through 1937 into 1938, though both were steadily lessening. The almost universal desire throughout the country was for the preservation of peace, though opinions differed as to the method by which that object was to be attained. In Chamberlain's view collective security was finished: "If I am right, as I am confident I am, in saying that the League as constituted to-day is unable to provide collective security for anybody, then I say we must not try to delude ourselves, and, still more, we must not try to delude small weak nations, into thinking that they will be protected by the League against aggression and acting accordingly, when we know that nothing of the kind can be expected."[2] Peace could therefore be preserved only by the reasonable settlement of matters in dispute through the normal processes of diplomacy. Chamberlain accordingly bent his efforts to the making of diplomatic contacts in Berlin and Rome with a view to establishing the bases of a settlement. In the case of Italy, as was shown in the previous chapter, he was willing to recognize Abyssinia and accept a Franco victory in Spain. In the case of Germany he admitted the need for changes in Austria, in the Sudeten German areas of Czechoslovakia, and in Danzig and the Polish Corridor, though only gradually did he reveal how far he was prepared to go. He was willing to consider Nazi claims in these regions, for on Versailles' own principle of self-determination Germany's grievances were legi-

---

[1] In a broadcast on the evening of Tuesday, 27 September, quoted in Wheeler-Bennett, J. W., *Munich, Prologue to Tragedy*, p. 157. Macmillan, 1948.
[2] *Parly. Debs.*, Fifth Series, H. of C., Vol. 332, col. 227.

timate: moreover he was fully confident in himself and his policy and had little trust in other countries or in the Labour opposition. As he wrote to his sister on 20 March 1938: "... with a French government in which one cannot have the slightest confidence and which I suspect to be in closish touch with our Opposition, with the Russians stealthily and cunningly pulling all the strings behind the scenes to get us involved in war with Germany (our Secret Service doesn't spend all its time looking out of the window) ... the prospect looked black indeed."[1]

With these conclusions the British ambassador at Berlin, Sir Nevile Henderson, cordially agreed. Chamberlain's Foreign Secretary, Eden, however, while not dissenting from the aims of his senior's policy, had different views about the methods necessary to their achievement. He did not believe in the piecemeal settlement of issues as they arose but rather in a general settlement either achieved through, or leading to the restoration of, an effective collective security system. He seems to have held the view that Germany and Italy were acting in close collusion, and therefore he saw no prospect of durability in a settlement with one and not the other. Moreover, he did not consider that a proper and lasting agreement could be made if concessions were to come from the side of the democracies only: if the Germans and Italians showed no disposition to compromise in any field, then the prospects of "normalized" relations could not appear to them very alluring. In these views he was sustained, and more than sustained, by Winston Churchill, who had made himself the leading spokesman of a small group of Conservatives who ceaselessly called attention to the character and danger of the new Nazi Reich, and to the unpreparedness of Britain to meet the threat. The Labour opposition still reserved more of their hatred for Mussolini than for Hitler, but, under the pressure of the Trades Union Congress led by Walter Citrine and Ernest Bevin, the Labour party was slowly beginning to understand the nature of Nazism and was therefore gradually coming to recognize the necessity for some measure of rearmament, and for closer relations with France. By the beginning of 1938, therefore, in contrast to 1936, the leading spirits in the government, perhaps with the exception of the Foreign Secretary, were rather more willing to consider meeting

[1] Quoted in Feiling, K., *The Life of Neville Chamberlain*, p. 347. Macmillan, 1946.

Germany half-way than the leaders of the opposition. The difference between the two parties on this issue was, however, at that date only small, and neither party was united in its views.

The differences between Chamberlain and Eden were brought to a head by developments in Austro-German relations in February. During a visit to Rome in the previous November Ribbentrop had found Mussolini by no means determined in his protection of Austrian independence, and early in the new year Hitler seems to have decided to test international reactions to a forward move. On 4 February Ribbentrop became Foreign Minister in place of Neurath and Hitler himself replaced Blomberg as Commander-in-Chief of the armed forces, the office of War Minister being abolished, and Keitel being appointed as chief of Hitler's personal staff. On 12 February the Austrian Chancellor Schuschnigg was summoned to Berchtesgaden and was there subjected to a tirade of abuse for his attitude towards Germany and to the Austrian Nazis. He was ordered within three days to promulgate an amnesty for the Austrian Nazis and to bring them into his government coalition party, the Patriotic Front: in particular, Seyss-Inquart was to be made Minister of Public Security.

This evident threat to Austrian independence at last gave Chamberlain an effective bargaining weapon to use both against Italy and against his own Foreign Secretary. Hitherto the Anglo-Italian conversations which Chamberlain desired to open and to which Eden was opposed without an earnest of Italian good faith had not appeared sufficiently urgent to justify forcing the issue in the British Cabinet; but Chamberlain judged, and judged correctly, that Austria would force the Italians to move, and would leave Eden almost alone in holding out against conversations. On 16 February Ciano wrote to Grandi instructing him to make clear to the British government that if Anglo-Italian relations were to be settled, conversations to that end must be begun before an *Anschluss*, since otherwise "it would be impossible to prevent the entire world interpreting our policy of *rapprochement* with London as a journey to Canossa under German pressure". In his letter Ciano insisted, disingenuously, that Mussolini was not "any more anxious today than yesterday to grasp the English by the hand" but "should the Nazi march into Austria in the meantime make its final advance and present us with a *fait accompli*, then there would exist no alternative and we would have to direct our policy in a spirit of sharp, open, immutable hostility towards the Western Powers".[1] With this letter in his pocket Grandi accepted Chamberlain's invitation to call at Downing Street on 18 February, and Grandi's report to Ciano says that at this interview Chamberlain and Eden were forging their weapons for their coming struggle in Cabinet. It is a fantastic account— Prime Minister and Foreign Secretary arguing in the presence of a foreign ambassador about the conditions upon which conversations with that ambassador's government might be opened; the Prime Minister asking leading questions of the ambassador to confound his own Foreign Minister (had Italy assented to the *Anschluss* in return for German support to Italian designs in the Mediterranean and in Europe?—to which, of course, Grandi, correctly, said: "No")—but the essential point here is Grandi's statement that neither Chamberlain nor Eden had any intention of resisting Germany in Austria. If this opinion were correct it would mean that Chamberlain was concerned to use the threat of the *Anschluss* merely as a means of forcing Italy to open conversations and of forcing Eden to agree, for Chamberlain had begun the interview by emphasizing the danger in Austria and pressing Grandi to state the position of the Italian government. Chamberlain's policy would have had a sounder foundation if he had been in fact bent on breaking the Axis over Austria, and Grandi's opinion about his real intentions could hardly be accepted in the absence of confirmatory evidence. But the evidence is there, first in Chamberlain's unwillingness, and Eden's willingness, to accede to the French Foreign Minister's proposal for a joint *démarche* in Berlin calling attention to the interest of Britain and France in Austrian independence; and secondly in the agenda prepared by Britain for the conversations with Italy after Eden's resignation but before the *Anschluss*, in which Austria was not mentioned.[2] It seems therefore clear that Chamberlain was in fact interested in the threat to Austria only as a means of forcing the issue of conversations with Italy both with Mussolini and with Eden: he

[1] Muggeridge, M. (ed.), *Ciano's Diplomatic Papers*, pp. 161-2. Odhams, 1948.
[2] *Ibid.*, pp. 189-91.

no doubt would have preferred Eden to have stayed in the Cabinet, but he was sufficiently intent on restoring good relations with Italy to accept Eden's resignation if there were no other way.

Eden's resignation from the government on 20 February was thus of great significance for the development of British policy. The two immediate issues were whether or not to join with France in warning Germany of Anglo-French interest in Austria and whether to open conversations with Italy before the latter country had evidenced her good faith by withdrawing from Spain and conforming to her professed policy of non-intervention. But behind these two issues lay the far greater question of the method by which an easement of the European situation should be sought. So convinced was Chamberlain of the correctness of his method, and so confident in his own ability to carry it through, that in January, in the absence abroad of Eden, he had reacted unfavourably to an enquiry from Washington about the British government's attitude to a plan then being considered by Roosevelt and Sumner Welles. The plan contemplated the summoning of a conference of neutral nations including the United States to draft a statement of the principles that should govern international relations, the methods by which international agreements might be peacefully revised, and the rights of neutrals in war. The statement was then to be presented to all nations for their consideration.[1] Despite Welles's warning that an unfavourable response might result in the destruction of American confidence in Britain, Chamberlain replied by saying that the British government was hopeful of appeasing Italy and Germany and he feared that Roosevelt's proposal might cut across his efforts. "That Mr. Chamberlain", comments Churchill, "with his limited outlook and inexperience of the European scene, should have possessed the self-sufficiency to wave away the proffered hand stretched out across the Atlantic leaves one, even at this date, breathless with amazement."[2] After his return to this country Eden did what he could to repair the damage, but it was too late and the American initiative was not renewed. The incident afforded, however, the

---

[1] Langer, W. L. and Gleason, S. E., *The Challenge to Isolation 1937-1940*, pp. 19-26. R.I.I.A., 1952.
[2] Churchill, W. S., *The Gathering Storm*, p. 199.

most striking demonstration of the depth of the gulf between the Prime Minister and the Foreign Secretary. To the one, the mere possibility even of the slightest American participation in a general settlement gave new hope: to the other, the American proposal for the formulation of general principles of international conduct cut across his attempt to settle issues piecemeal according to his own view of the merits of each case.

The course of British policy was now set. The attempt was to be made for appeasement in Europe by satisfying German and Italian grievances to the extent that Chamberlain and his immediate circle of advisers considered them legitimate. On 3 March Henderson had an interview with Hitler in order to enquire into the prospects for disarmament, for a peaceful settlement of the Austrian problem, and for meeting Germany's colonial demands through some sort of colonial consortium. Hitler showed himself almost wholly intransigent. On 9 March Schuschnigg suddenly announced his intention of holding on 13 March a plebiscite on Austrian independence. On the next day the Chautemps-Delbos government in Paris resigned. Hitler reacted with his usual brilliant opportunism, and on 11 March a series of ultimatums was delivered by Goering over the telephone to Vienna—first for the cancellation of the plebiscite, then for the resignation of Schuschnigg, then for the appointment of Seyss-Inquart as Chancellor, then for a request from Seyss-Inquart for German troops to enter Austria to maintain law and order. Mussolini, faced with the fateful decision, hid himself away in his country villa. Ciano refused to receive the British and French ambassadors if their object in seeking an interview was to discuss Austria. The acting French Foreign Minister Delbos could evoke no great concern in London. Schuschnigg, appealing desperately to the British government for advice, received the chilling reply: "His Majesty's Government cannot take responsibility of advising the Chancellor to take any course of action which might expose his country to dangers against which His Majesty's Government are unable to guarantee protection."[1] Ribbentrop, in London on a short visit, reported that information of a German ultimatum had produced a lively reaction from the new Foreign

[1] Woodward, E. L. and Butler, R., *Documents on British Foreign Policy, 1919-1939*, Third Series, Vol. I, p. 13.

Secretary, Halifax, who suggested the holding of a plebiscite in Austria under international control like that in the Saar in 1935; but Chamberlain, who appeared calm and cool-headed, said that the situation did not require such a plebiscite—he personally understood the position, but British public opinion would hardly accept a settlement of the question in effect by force.[1] Bereft of support from any of the three major powers, Schuschnigg and the Austrian President, Miklas, had no course but to submit, and the transformation of Austria into a province of the German Reich was formally proclaimed on 13 March. The British government's only action was to register in Berlin a formal protest against "use of coercion backed by force against an independent State in order to create a situation incompatible with its national independence".[2]

The *Anschluss* greatly improved Hitler's chances of successful action against Czechoslovakia. To the continuing Spanish factor was now added the presence of German troops on the Brenner to hold Mussolini in the German camp. The weakness of Britain and France had been revealed. Czechoslovakia was strategically outflanked. The concern felt in Moscow was demonstrated on 17 March when the Foreign Commissar, Litvinov, proposed that the powers interested in preventing further aggression should consult together on the practical measures called for by the circumstances. The official reply to this proposal on 24 March aptly summed up Chamberlain's policy: "A conference only attended by some of the European Powers, and designed less to secure the settlement of outstanding problems than to organise concerted action against aggression, would not necessarily . . . have such a favourable effect upon the prospects of European peace."[3] In his speech in the House of Commons on the same day Chamberlain buttressed his rejection of the Soviet proposal by saying that definite assurances had been received from Germany about the integrity of Czechoslovakia. This was not strictly accurate, for the German assurances had stated merely that Germany would continue her policy of improving

---

[1] *Documents on German Foreign Policy, 1918-1945*, Series D., Vol. I, pp. 274-5. H.M.S.O., 1949.
[2] Woodward, E. L. and Butler, R., *Documents on British Foreign Policy, 1919-1939*, Third Series, Vol. I, p. 25.
[3] *Ibid.*, p. 101.

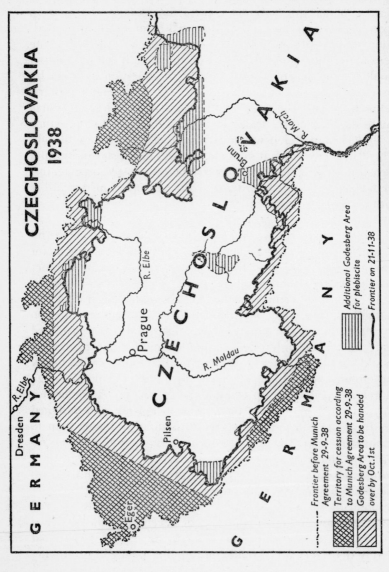

This map approximately indicates how by the frontier finally agreed on 21 November, Czechoslovakia ceded more territory than Hitler had demanded at Godesberg for immediate cession. Most of the Godesberg plebiscite areas, however, remained in Czech hands.

German-Czech relations and that the German-Czech arbitration treaty of 1925 was still adhered to by Germany. The difference of view between the U.S.S.R. and Britain about the nature of the German threat and the way to meet it was, however, epitomized in this exchange—the Soviet view that aggression could be stopped and peace secured only by a strong coalition of the non-Fascist powers, and the British opinion that peace was to be secured by discussing the issues with the aggrieved powers and meeting their legitimate grievances. A similar divergence of view was to appear in the negotiations with the Soviet Union in 1939. Some members of the British government might have been less confident in Chamberlain's method had they known of a secret conference in Berlin on 28 March attended by Hitler, Hess, Ribbentrop and the leaders of the Sudeten German party in Czechoslovakia, at which Hitler gave instructions for the conduct of negotiations between the Sudeten Germans and the Czech government. These instructions were summarized by the Sudeten German leader, Henlein, in the words: "We must always demand so much that we can never be satisfied."[1] Chamberlain himself, however, would probably not have been deterred from his purpose of achieving a peaceful settlement of the Czech question, though he would have been more aware of the difficulty of his task, for he had already made up his mind that Britain could not defend Czechoslovakia. In the letter to his sister on 20 March already quoted he wrote: "You have only to look at the map to see that nothing that France or we could do could possibly save Czechoslovakia from being overrun by the Germans, if they wanted to do it. The Austrian frontier is practically open; the great Skoda munition works are within easy bombing distance of the German aerodromes, the railways all pass through German territory, Russia is 100 miles away. . . . I have therefore abandoned any idea of giving guarantees to Czechoslovakia, or the French in connection with her [*sic*] obligations to that country."[2]

The main decisions of policy had then been taken by the end of March. Hitler was determined on the destruction of Czechoslovakia, using as his tool and pretext the Sudeten German minority within the country. Chamberlain had decided that he

---

[1] *Documents on German Foreign Policy, 1918-1945*, Series D, Vol. II, p. 198.
[2] Quoted in Feiling, K., *The Life of Neville Chamberlain*, pp. 347-8.

could not defend Czechoslovakia and that he would not go to war on the Czech issue. For this reason, and because of the general distrust of the U.S.S.R. felt by the British government, the Soviet proposal for a conference against aggression had been rebuffed. There remained the problem of France, for France had explicit treaty obligations to defend Czechoslovakia against aggression, and if France became involved in war with Germany on account of Czechoslovakia, and were seriously menaced by Germany, then it would be impossible for Britain to stand aside. The task of British policy then was to bring simultaneous pressure in Berlin, in Prague and in Paris—in Berlin to keep the Sudeten demands as moderate as possible so that the Czechs could accept them, in Prague to make the Czechs yield to the Sudeten demands so that Hitler would not need to attack and therefore the Franco-Czech treaty would not become operative, and in Paris to obtain French agreement to this policy so that the Czechs would not be encouraged to hold out. Pressure in Berlin was inevitably fruitless since Hitler had made up his mind: the satisfaction that this decision gave him is illustrated by the opening sentence of his military directive of 30 May: "It is my unalterable decision to smash Czechoslovakia by military action in the near future".[1] If the policy were to succeed, therefore, it was in fact reduced to forcing Czechoslovakia to accept whatever the Sudetens and Hitler demanded, and persuading France to join in this compulsion.

Shortly after the *Anschluss* an indication of the British attitude to the Czech question was given in a memorandum to the French government, and early consultation was proposed. Accordingly the French Prime Minister, Daladier, and the Foreign Minister, Bonnet, came to London for a conference on 28 and 29 April. Chamberlain, supported by Halifax, there set out the British views that effective military assistance to Czechoslovakia was impossible, that British public opinion would never support a war to prevent the self-determination of a central European minority, and that the question could be settled within the framework of the Czech state. He assured the French ministers that the Czech President, Benesh, would not be pressed to accept terms which meant the destruction of his country, but he refused to promise support to Benesh if the

---

[1] *Documents on German Foreign Policy, 1918-1945*, Series D, Vol. II, p. 358.

latter made all the concessions demanded of him and Germany none the less attacked, because the action of the British government in hypothetical circumstances could not be pledged in advance. The intentions of the British government, though wrapped up in diplomatic language, and though their ultimate implications may well not have been foreseen, were thus made perfectly clear to the French. The French Foreign Minister seized upon the British arguments and pressed his reluctant Premier along the road of appeasement. It was agreed that the staff talks that had been begun in 1936 should be extended, that the two countries should bring joint pressure on Benesh to make the utmost possible concessions in liberalizing the position of the Sudetens in Czechoslovakia, and that Britain alone should ask Germany to abstain from pressure while the Czech-Sudeten negotiations were proceeding. If developments should seem to make it necessary, Britain should also warn Germany in the terms of the Prime Minister's speech in the House on 24 March, that if war should break out, it was impossible to tell how far it might spread.

In the succeeding months unremitting pressure was brought to bear on the Czechs by Britain to speed up concessions to the Sudetens, while German threats and insults mounted. France was urged also to press the Czechs to move faster, and Bonnet needed little encouragement. But early in July the possibility of a breakdown in the Czech-Sudeten negotiations emerged, and Britain then suggested that Benesh might ask for an independent British mediator to reach a settlement. Benesh was deeply shocked at what he considered intervention in the internal affairs of his country, but in order not to lose British good-will he did as he was asked, and the mission of Lord Runciman was announced on 25 July. Runciman successfully exposed the fraud of the negotiations, for although he persuaded Benesh to agree to almost all that the Sudetens had demanded, the Sudetens broke off the negotiations on the pretext of an incident in the frontier region. In a speech at the Nuremberg party rally on 12 September Hitler demanded self-determination for the Sudetens and declared Germany to be a nation in arms. He was no doubt encouraged to pursue his course by a leader that had appeared in *The Times* on 7 September, the last paragraph of which included the words: "it might be worth while for the Czechoslovak

Government to consider whether they should exclude altogether the project, which has found favour in some quarters, of making Czechoslovakia a more homogeneous State by the secession of that fringe of alien populations who are contiguous to the nation with which they are united by race".[1]

Hitler's speech had three immediate results. There was a revolt in the Sudetenland, which the Czechs swiftly suppressed after proclaiming martial law. French morale suddenly collapsed in face of the choice between defaulting on their obligations or going to war if the Czechs stood firm. Chamberlain sent a cable to Hitler proposing coming to Germany to see him with a view to trying to find a peaceful solution. The idea had been discussed with Henderson and a few members of the government two weeks previously, but the telegram was actually sent without the Cabinet being consulted.[2]

All the world wished Chamberlain well in his mission of pacification, though the Czechs feared that the fact of his journey signified British determination to prevent war, which meant, given Hitler's present mood, forcing Czechoslovakia to surrender. The Chancellor and the Prime Minister met at Berchtesgaden on 15 September, with only the German interpreter, Schmidt, present at the interview. Hitler made it clear by implication that he was bent on the destruction of Czechoslovakia, but professed himself willing to discuss ways and means of implementing the principle of self-determination for the Sudetens once the principle was accepted. Chamberlain expressed personal sympathy for the principle but said he could not agree without consulting his colleagues; but he in effect bowed to force by accepting Hitler's refusal to join with him in an appeal to both sides in Czechoslovakia for moderation. Chamberlain then returned to Britain to explain the position to his colleagues and to Daladier and Bonnet, who came over to London on 18 September. At this conference Chamberlain insisted that only self-determination for the Sudetens would prevent war, and after a show of strength and an adjournment

[1] It was believed at the time by the German embassy, and by many others in this country, that this leader was written after consultation between Chamberlain and the editor, who were close personal friends. This belief is now known to have been mistaken. See *The History of The Times, Vol. IV*, "The 150th Anniversary and Beyond", Part II, pp. 929-33. P.H.S., 1952.
[2] Feiling, K., *The Life of Neville Chamberlain*, p. 363.

Daladier agreed that some cession of territory was necessary. The conference then agreed to propose that territory the population of which was more than fifty per cent German should be ceded by Czechoslovakia either directly or after a plebiscite, that the frontiers should be adjusted and an exchange of populations arranged by an international commission including a representative of Czechoslovakia, and that Britain and France would join in an international guarantee of the new boundaries of Czechoslovakia against unprovoked aggression—this guarantee being in substitution for Czechoslovakia's existing mutual assistance treaties. The conference was concerned to determine only the general principles of a settlement, and the plan was vague in its details: the British and French imagined that these could be settled by the international commission by amicable discussion round a table. Chamberlain's flight to Munich had, however, produced a revolutionary change in British policy: Britain was now offering to join in guaranteeing a central European state—a commitment that she had consistently refused to undertake throughout the inter-war years, and the refusal of which had been a main cause of dispute with France. It was indeed a somewhat fantastic procedure—to strip a country of the strategic frontier and the powerful fortifications without which it could not defend itself, and then to guarantee the defenceless rump. All was staked on Hitler's good faith.

The Czechs not unnaturally understood the danger. On 20 September they replied objecting to the plan on economic, strategic and constitutional grounds, and suggesting recourse to the arbitration treaty of 1925. The British and French ministers in Prague were, however, unofficially informed that the Czech reply might be modified if pressure were brought to bear, and the two representatives were therefore instructed by their governments to inform Benesh that if the Anglo-French plan were rejected and Czechoslovakia were subsequently attacked by Germany, Britain and France would stand aside. In the late afternoon of 21 September the Czechs accordingly replied that, under "excessively urgent pressure", they accepted the Anglo-French proposals in the understanding that the territory to be ceded would remain Czech until the final frontier had been fixed by the international commission, and that until then Britain and France would allow no German invasion. This was the vital point, for if German troops occupied the frontier defences before the new frontier was delimited and guaranteed, the representatives on the international commission would have no defence against the pressure of the German delegate, backed by the German army, for wide cessions of territory.

Elated with his success in obtaining the acquiescence of France and the submission of the Czechs, and thereby, as he thought, a peaceful settlement of the problem, Chamberlain flew to Godesberg on 22 September to lay the Anglo-French plan before Hitler. There, to his astonishment and anger, he found that Hitler had prepared his own plan for implementing the principle of self-determination. The territory agreed for cession should be occupied by 1 October at the latest; Germany would participate in no international guarantee of the new state until Polish and Hungarian claims had been satisfied; and plebiscites should be held under German control in all disputed areas on the model of the Saar plebiscite (which meant that Germans who had left the territory since 1918 could vote and Czechs who had entered it could not—thus showing that Hitler was interested not in the Germans longing to return to the Reich, but in territory). There was bitter disputation between the two men. Chamberlain agreed to put the proposals to the Czechs without any recommendation. On 25 September the Czechs rejected them unconditionally.

The crisis had now reached its height. The French Ministers again made their journey to London, and on the morning of the 26th the two governments agreed that if the Germans attacked and the Czechs resisted, France would have to support them and Britain would come in with France. This agreement was announced by the Foreign Office in the afternoon. On the same evening Hitler spoke with hysterical violence in the *Sportpalast* in Berlin, and publicly announced 1 October as his date for entry into Czechoslovakia. Chamberlain had, however, not entirely lost hope, and with Daladier's agreement he had that morning despatched his personal adviser, Sir Horace Wilson, to Berlin with a letter to Hitler pointing out that the only disagreement was one of method. In the afternoon Wilson was instructed to warn Hitler that an attack on Czechoslovakia would bring in France and then Britain; but in view of Hitler's hysterical condition before the *Sportpalast* speech, Wilson delayed the warning until the following morning. When the interview took place Hitler remained intransigent and demanded Czech acceptance of the Godesberg proposals by 2 p.m. the next day, the 28th. He promised to reply to Chamberlain's letter, however, and the reply contained just sufficient to induce Chamberlain to make one last effort although the British fleet had already been mobilized. On the morning of the 28th he sent a further message to Hitler offering to come once more to Germany to discuss the issue with the Germans and the Czechs, and with the French and the Italians if Hitler so desired. At the same time he instructed the British ambassador in Rome, Lord Perth, to press Mussolini to support the idea of a conference. This the Italian dictator agreed to do, and his intervention with Hitler proved successful. Invitations to a four-power conference at Munich (not including the Czechs) were immediately sent out, and Chamberlain received the information as he was about to conclude the account of the crisis and his activities that he was giving to a specially summoned House of Commons. He accepted the invitation on the spot, the House went into a delirium of relief, and Attlee agreed to the adjournment of the House till 3 October (two days after Hitler's deadline). Sinclair for the Liberals asked Chamberlain to safeguard the political and economic independence of Czechoslovakia, and only Gallacher, the lone Communist member, protested against the forcible dismemberment of a friendly democratic country. But Eden walked out of the chamber in disgust, and Harold Nicolson remained seated amid the chaos and pandemonium around him.

At the time the Munich conference assembled, the Czechs had accepted the principles of cession of the Sudeten German regions contained in the Anglo-French plan, together with the idea of an international conference at which, of course, they were to be represented, and an outline time-table for the cession subject to the basic reservation about no evacuation of the fortified zones until the frontier was fixed. Chamberlain had objected to the Godesberg proposals only because he felt he could not justify such an open display of force to British public opinion, and also perhaps because his own faith in Hitler had been in some degree shaken by his reception at Godesberg; but he was careless of the actual fate of Czechoslovakia, and now that the spectre of war that had seemed so close had been temporarily banished, he was determined that it should not be allowed to reappear. There was no danger that agreement would not be reached at Munich, as the Czechs clearly recognized. The agreement was dated 29 September but was actually signed in the early hours of 30 September. The boundaries of four zones were described on a map, evacuation of these zones by the Czechs to begin on 1 October and to be completed by 10 October leaving intact "existing installations". The four zones were to be occupied in defined stages by German troops beginning on 1 October and ending on 10 October. An international commission including a Czech representative was to be established to determine for occupation by 10 October the remaining territory of predominantly German character. The commission should determine zones in which plebiscites should be held, under the same conditions as those governing the Saar plebiscite. As a result of pressure by Daladier, the commission was given power to recommend minor modifications in the strictly ethnic delimitation of the frontier. To the agreement were attached four annexes: that Britain and France stood by their offer relating to an international guarantee of the new boundaries against unprovoked aggression, and Germany and Italy would give guarantees when the Polish and Hungarian minority questions were settled; that a new four-power meeting on the Polish and Hungarian minority problems should be held if they had not been settled within three months; that the commission should have power to deal with all questions arising out of the transfer; and that the commission should consist of the German State Secretary, Weizsäcker; the British, French and Italian ambassadors in Berlin, Henderson, François-Poncet and Attolico; and a Czech representative. The agreement was presented to the Czechs by Daladier and Chamberlain, Daladier being nervous, ill at ease and ashamed, while Chamberlain, tired but satisfied, yawned and was clearly anxious to get away to bed.

Chamberlain, and to his astonishment Daladier, were received with rapturous applause on returning to their own countries. On the morning of 30 September Chamberlain had used the favourable atmosphere produced by Munich to gain Hitler's signature to a declaration that Britain and Germany would consult together on problems mutually concerning them, and that Munich and the Anglo-German naval agreement symbolized the desire of the two peoples never again to go to war with one another. This declaration was no doubt much in the Premier's mind when in an unguarded moment on the evening of the same day he announced to the cheering crowd outside Downing Street, "this is the second time in our history that there has come back from Germany to Downing Street peace with honour. I believe it is peace for our time."[1] But the mood of elation was soon to pass. Duff Cooper resigned his position in the Cabinet as First Lord of the Admiralty and in a ringing speech in the House denounced the agreement, the surrender of Europe to domination by a single power, and the morality that could effect such a betrayal as that of the Czechs. Churchill spoke of the total and unmitigated defeat suffered by Britain and France; the opposition condemned Chamberlain's surrender to force (but evaded the question of whether they would have gone to war by saying that Hitler was bluffing—which he was not); all parties agreed that the pace of British rearmament must be increased. In the international commission established by Munich the Czechs, usually supported by François-Poncet, often by Attolico, and occasionally by Henderson, protested against the extortions of Weizsäcker, but after their fortified zones were occupied they had no defence: they agreed to negotiate directly with the Germans on zone five, so plebiscites were not held and international troops were not necessary; after German threats of force on 5 October, the 1910 census, which was known to exaggerate the numbers of Germans, was used to decide the areas whose population was more than fifty per cent German; Daladier's clause about modification of the strictly ethnic frontier was interpreted to favour Germany, not Czechoslovakia as he had intended; the German definition of "intact installations" was accepted; the Hungarian claims were settled by a German-Italian decision on 2 November, and Britain and France were not consulted (though Britain was not displeased to be absolved from participation in a further distasteful decision); Germany and Italy never guaranteed the new Czech frontiers, so the international guarantee never came into existence.

The apologists for Munich based their case on six main propo-

[1] Quoted in Wheeler-Bennett, J. W., *Munich, Prologue to Tragedy,* pp. 180-1.

sitions. Britain and France could not bring effective or sufficiently early military assistance to save Czechoslovakia from being overrun, and neither could the Soviet Union, if indeed she intended to, because of the Polish and Rumanian refusals to allow Soviet troops to cross their territory. There was no moral ground for opposing self-determination. British and French public opinion would never have supported war for Czechoslovakia or against self-determination. The Dominions, especially South Africa, Canada and Australia, were at best reluctant to fight on such an issue, at worst determined to stay neutral. No sufficient evidence yet existed to show that a preventive war was necessary—and if a preventive war were to be fought this was not morally the issue nor militarily the time to select, for British and French rearmament was only just beginning. Finally, war now had been avoided.

These arguments were countered by a different set of propositions. Hitler was bluffing. The Czechs were betrayed. The issue was not self-determination or the integrity of Czechoslovakia, but whether or not Britain was to allow the continent of Europe to fall under the domination of a Germany ruled by a semi-maniac and inspired by a philosophy of barbarism. The loss of Czechoslovakia, and consequently of her other eastern allies, gravely weakened France and therefore Britain, while Germany gained control of the strategic citadel of central Europe, and of large and valuable raw materials and industrial resources.

Thus the protagonists on both sides failed to answer the contentions of their opponents in a dispute that was argued with more bitterness and intensity than any other political issue of the inter-war years. Some of the propositions can now be confirmed or refuted: others will remain a source of controversy. Militarily Britain and France were weak, but so was Germany: the German forces covering the French frontier were so light that they could have been brushed aside if the French army had been ordered to attack, and the French army could not have been checked unless the German army and air force had been called off from its attack on Czechoslovakia. If the Soviet air force had been thrown into the fray, the war might well have been over fairly swiftly. The imponderables in this argument are whether the U.S.S.R. would have joined in, and whether the

French army would have attacked. The British government had good reason for doubts on both these counts, but more particularly the latter. The "gaining-time-for-rearmament" argument is valid only if it is also argued that Poland should have been abandoned in 1939, for Germany increased her armed strength by September 1939 very much more than Britain and France increased theirs in the same period. Public opinion overwhelmingly supported Munich after the agreement was signed, but this is not to say that the people would not have recognized the necessity of war had the issue been presented to them in its proper terms: both Kordt of the German embassy and Henderson noticed the hardening of public opinion after 25 September when the government's lead slightly changed. On the other hand the government was right in believing that Hitler was not bluffing and failure to accept his terms would have meant war. In making that correct judgment, Chamberlain could not but give the greatest weight to the moral collapse of France and to the attitude of the Dominions.

The word "Munich" has now come to stand in the English language as a symbol for national humiliation and betrayal. For that humiliation the whole British people, and the French, and indeed in some degree the American, must bear some part of the blame. The peoples had allowed their morale and morality to be sapped and destroyed by the First World War, by the World Economic Crisis, and by the depression and international disputes of the 'thirties, so that the governments that ruled over them (with the exception of the administration, though not the Congress, in Washington) reflected their lack of principle, their selfishness, or their apathy. Chamberlain inherited the results of his predecessors' weaknesses, and the pursuit of expediency to the exclusion of principle was carried by him to a point where continental Europe was engulfed and Britain herself tottered on the brink of destruction. The real issue at Munich was not the self-determination of the Sudetens or even the fate of Czechoslovakia: it was whether or not the political, social and moral way of life which was western civilization, and to which Britain claimed to adhere, was to be defended. Even if all his agents' reports had been insufficient, Chamberlain, had he thought in those terms, could hardly have failed to realize when he came face to face with Hitler that here

M 149

was an enemy. In that case war would have been joined in 1938 instead of 1939 on a better strategic ground, in a stronger comparative state of armaments,[1] with a greater chance of Soviet co-operation, with Germany's access to essential raw materials barred, with Italy still embroiled in Spain, and with a conscience unburdened by a sense of shame and betrayal. Munich was the greatest moral defeat suffered by Britain in this century, and the effects of it are still by no means ended.[2]

[1] With the one small but vital exception of the expansion of Britain's air fighter force between 1938 and 1939.

[2] No consideration has been given in this chapter to the German army plot to overthrow Hitler in September 1938, which was abandoned on receipt of news of Chamberlain's intervention. The British government was aware of the existence of the plot, but this knowledge could hardly be decisive one way or the other when balanced against the weighty considerations on both sides of the case which are set out above. The later history of the German resistance does not inspire confidence that the plot would have succeeded had the attempt been made.

Chapter 12

THE POLISH CRISIS AND WAR

In the judgment of the former Rumanian Foreign Minister, Grigore Gafencu, Poland was less suitable as a rallying point for European solidarity than any other country.[1] She had had links with Hitler since the non-aggression pact of January 1934; she had flirted with Hungary's revisionist aspirations in the Balkans; she had participated in the onslaught on Czechoslovakia in the autumn of 1938; she possessed a large area of White Russian and Ukrainian territory which the U.S.S.R. was bent on regaining; she had set little store by the principles of the League Covenant, and had attempted to undermine the control of the League High Commissioner in Danzig; her internal régime was of a semi-dictatorial character; strategically she suffered from interrupted communications and the absence of natural frontiers. Had the matter been presented in 1939 as the defence of Danzig or the Polish Corridor, Poland would have had little moral claim to assistance. The matter was not so presented, for the British government had at last realized that the question at issue was whether or not the whole of Europe, perhaps even including Britain herself, was to fall under the control of Nazi Germany.

The eyes of Chamberlain had been opened to this unpleasant fact by Hitler's seizure of Prague and Bratislava in March 1939. The previous six months had seen minor alarums and excursions on the international field, but no major crisis. But on 21 October Hitler had secretly signed a directive for the occupation of the remainder of Bohemia and Moravia, and at the Wilhelmstrasse Ribbentrop had opened conversations with the Polish ambassador, Lipski, about the retrocession of Danzig to the Reich and the opening of an extraterritorial road and rail communications-link across the Polish Corridor to join East Prussia to the Reich. On 24 November Hitler had ordered the preparation of plans for the seizure of Danzig during exploitation of a revolutionary

[1] Gafencu, G., *Prelude to the Russian Campaign*, p. 233. Muller, 1945.

situation, and not as part of a war with Poland; but the Polish–
German discussions had not hitherto been marked by any
serious German pressure against the Polish unwillingness to

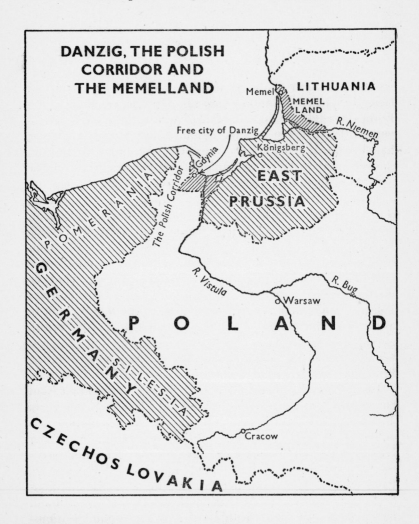

consider more than minor modifications in Danzig or in the
Corridor. It seems that Hitler in this period was hesitating
before the various possibilities open to him—occupation of the
remainder of the now-federal Czecho-Slovakia, a move against

Danzig or Poland, seizure of the Memelland, or a direct attack on France. His mind may well have been made up for him by the success of his agents' fomenting of Slovak separatist sentiment against the Czechs. The Prague government's dismissal of the Slovak government in Bratislava for its separatist activities on 9 March set in train the course of events by which first the Slovak Premier, Tiso, then the Czech President, Hacha, were summoned to Berlin and forced to ask Hitler to take their countries under his protection, while Hungary was given the green light to go ahead with the long-desired occupation of the Ruthenian tip of Czecho-Slovakia. German troops were in Prague on 15 March and in Bratislava on 16 March. On 22 March Lithuania submitted to an ultimatum from Berlin and surrendered the Memelland. On 23 March Rumania signed with Germany a far-reaching trade treaty which gave Germany a considerable measure of control over the Rumanian economy. The foundations of the European edifice were visibly crumbling away.

The British government's reaction to these events was initially cautious. In October a government spokesman had said that Britain regarded herself as morally bound by the guarantee to Czecho-Slovakia, although the guarantee was not formally in existence; but now in answer to questions in the House Chamberlain said that the guarantee was against unprovoked aggression, and none such was known to have taken place. Halifax in the Lords said that the guarantee was never in fact in existence, and what had now occurred was an internal movement for independence; but he did admit that outside influences had been brought to bear and this was against the spirit if not the letter of Munich. But the time for the language of appeasement was past. There was a chorus of outraged hostility in the Press, and Halifax joined his professional advisers in insisting to Chamberlain that the wave of aggression must be halted. Chamberlain slowly faced the evidence that his whole past policy had been based on misjudgments and false assumptions, and on 17 March he spoke in public of the promises made to him personally which Hitler had now broken: what reliance could be placed on any assurances of Hitler in the future? was this the end of an old adventure or the beginning of a new? was this a step to world conquest?

The speed of events now mounted rapidly. Immediately after Prague the Rumanian minister in London made an alarmist statement to Halifax about German designs on Rumania, and a hurriedly prepared note was sent to the governments of eastern Europe and of France to ask whether they would support Rumania if she were threatened: the smaller countries all replied, not unnaturally, that a big factor in their decision would be the attitude of Great Britain. France replied in the affirmative. Moscow replied by suggesting a conference at Bucharest, but Halifax doubted whether a minister could be spared to go to Bucharest, and feared lest the conference should fail, in which case matters would be worse. In view of the replies from the other governments, a new proposal was now made on 20 March from London to Paris, Warsaw and Moscow that the four countries should sign and publish a declaration that they were about to consult on the steps necessary for joint resistance to any threat to the independence of a European state. France and the U.S.S.R. agreed, but Poland, fearing that open association with the Soviet Union might provoke a German attack against her, proposed a bilateral consultative agreement between Britain and Poland. The British and French Governments were now faced with a fateful decision—whether to stake everything on agreement with the Russians and possibly lose Poland, or whether to come to an understanding with Poland and hope to bring in the Soviet Union later. On 22 March they decided on the latter policy, partly because they minimized the military strength of the U.S.S.R. and over-estimated that of Poland and Rumania, partly because Rumania seemed the country immediately threatened and Rumania was allied to France and to Poland and did not want Soviet assistance, partly because they were not sure if they could quickly get a satisfactory agreement with the Soviet government, and partly because they considered Poland and Rumania had perhaps some reason for fearing that if the Red army once entered their territory it might never leave. Anglo-French proposals to assist Poland and Rumania under certain conditions were accordingly made to Warsaw and Bucharest on 27 March, but on the next day fears in London that Germany might be planning a sudden *coup* were greatly heightened by news of a German Press onslaught on Poland, and by unofficial information from various sources that Poland was the next item on Germany's programme. In point of fact no such *coup* was planned but—although the Poles dod not so inform the British or the French—on 21 March Ribbentrop had suddenly renewed his demand for Danzig and an extraterritorial corridor across the Corridor, on 26 March Lipski had made counter-proposals excluding extraterritoriality or the cession of Danzig, on 27 March Ribbentrop had ominously said that Polish-German relations were suffering serious deterioration, and the next day the Polish Foreign Minister Beck had replied that any change in the *status quo* at Danzig brought about by the Reich would be considered by Poland as aggression against herself.

Ignorant of these exchanges, but fearful that something was afoot and they would again be too late, the British Cabinet met on 29 March and again on the 30th, and decided to ask Polish approval of a statement to be made by the Prime Minister in the House the next day to the effect that "in the event of any action which clearly threatened Polish independence, and which the Polish Government accordingly considered it vital to resist with their national forces, His Majesty's Government would feel themselves bound at once to lend the Polish Government all support in their power".[1] The telegram of instruction to the British ambassador in Warsaw was drafted in Chamberlain's own hand.[2] Between two flicks of the ash off his cigarette Beck made up his mind to accept.[3] The British ambassador's suggestion that the formula might be amended to read: "in the event of any *unprovoked* action" was rejected. It was indeed a grotesque situation. Ignorant of the state of affairs between the bully and the threatened victim, the power and destinies of the British people were placed at the command of a clique of Polish officer-states-men, whose courage was not in dispute, but whose record of international conduct was by no means of the highest; a com-mitment in eastern Europe, which the British government and the Dominions had steadfastly resisted, had been uncondition-ally accepted; the guarantee was strategically but words and breath without Soviet co-operation, but the refusal of the Soviet proposal for a conference, the summary dropping of the

---

[1] Woodward, E. L. and Butler, R., *Documents on British Foreign Policy, 1919-1939*, Third Series, Vol. IV, p. 552.

[2] *Ibid.*, p. 546.

[3] Namier, L. B., *Diplomatic Prelude, 1938-1939*, p. 107. Macmillan, 1948.

British government's own proposed four-power declaration to which the Soviet government had agreed, and the greater importance evidently attached to the friendship of a state hostile to the U.S.S.R., made that co-operation far more difficult of attainment. On 13 April similar guarantees were given to Greece—as a consequence of the Italian occupation of Albania on 7 April, and to convince Turkey of the Anglo-French determination to stand against further aggression—and also to Rumania, as a result of a personal appeal from Daladier. A provisional agreement on mutual assistance was concluded with Turkey on 12 May: Turkey wished to formalize the alliance only in association with the Soviet Union, and arrangements therefore hung fire during negotiations with Moscow. The pact was eventually signed without Soviet concurrence on 19 October, after the outbreak of war.

Having committed themselves to the maintenance of Polish and Rumanian independence, the British and French governments turned to the task of securing Soviet co-operation.[1] The task was formidable enough, for the Kremlin's ideological suspicion of capitalist states had been reinforced by the long chain of evidence of western complacence in Fascist expansionism not merely in East Africa, in Spain, in Austria and Czechoslovakia, but also in Manchuria and China, an area of at least equal importance to the U.S.S.R. Moreover, the Anglo-French guarantees to Poland and Rumania meant that Hitler could attack the Soviet Union without bringing in Britain and France only through the narrow corridor of the Baltic States, whereas a move by Hitler in almost any direction must involve the western powers; so that the Anglo-French negotiators had almost no additional security to offer to the Soviet Union in exchange for the Soviet support that they were now soliciting. By this time almost as distrustful of the west as of Hitler, the U.S.S.R. was determined that any agreement with the west should guarantee effective western participation in any Russo-German conflict: that meant a watertight alliance, arrangements to cover the Baltic gap, and military conversations which would co-ordinate plans and disclose the amount and quality

---

[1] The documentation for these negotiations is to be found in Woodward, E. L. and Butler, R., *Documents on British Foreign Policy, 1919-1939*, Third Series, Vols. V-VI, and in *Nazi-Soviet Relations, 1939-1941*.

of the Anglo-French military contributions. On the other hand, if satisfactory understandings on these matters could not be reached with Britain and France, the dreaded attack of Hitler and of Japan might be as effectively turned aside by making an agreement with the aggressors, and thereby adopting what they believed to be the Anglo-French policy of turning aggression away from themselves.

The British approached the conversations with the U.S.S.R. from a very different angle. The overriding British object was to gain an assurance of Soviet help in case of war, and, as we have seen, Britain had little to offer in exchange beyond the commitments she had already undertaken. Secondly, Britain was concerned not to offend the susceptibilities of Poland and Rumania, round whom the peace front was being built, and both of whom had good reason to fear the Soviet Union. Thirdly, Britain wished to do nothing to provoke a German attack which might otherwise not have been decided upon. Fourthly, Britain feared that too close an association with the power that controlled the Comintern might have a bad effect on world public opinion—might, in particular, drive a still-undecided Japan finally into the arms of Germany, with disastrous results for British interests in the Far East. Accordingly, the first serious proposals made to the Soviet Union since before the Polish guarantee were for unilateral Soviet guarantees to Poland and Rumania similar to those already given by Britain and France. On 17 April, within two days of the submission of the British suggestion, the Soviet government countered with a proposal for a tripartite mutual assistance treaty between Britain, France and the U.S.S.R., its terms to cover an attack against any one of the three, or against any east European country between Finland and the Black Sea.

The next six weeks were occupied by a succession of proposals designed to bridge the gap between these two totally opposed conceptions—Britain wishing to avoid provocation or the formation of a *bloc* with the Communists, and therefore suggesting independent guarantees of which those of the Soviet Union might if she wished be contingent on prior operation of the British and French; the U.S.S.R. desiring a tight alliance, which would leave Britain and France no loopholes, and which might possibly be strong enough to deter Hitler from attacking. At length on 27 May, under the urging of France, Britain agreed to a triple alliance against direct aggression to operate in conformity with the principles (not the procedure) of the League Covenant. In the meantime, however, there had been two ominous developments, one public, one secret. On 3 May the Jew Litvinov, the Moscow apostle of collective security, had suddenly been replaced as Commissar for Foreign Affairs by Molotov, a man deep in the inner workings of the Kremlin, but little versed in foreign affairs and ignorant of other countries. On 17 April the Soviet ambassador in Berlin had sought an interview with Weizsäcker, and had brought the conversation round to a point where he could ask Weizsäcker his views about German-Soviet relations. The Germans, wanting an economic agreement, cautiously responded; but Molotov on 20 May said that an economic agreement must rest on the necessary political bases: on 27 May the German Foreign Office was still of the opinion that the disadvantageous effects on Italy and Japan of a *rapprochement* with the Kremlin outweighed its advantages, but on 30 May Hitler decided, of course unknown to Moscow, that negotiations should be opened, though with the utmost caution.

On 2 June the U.S.S.R. answered the Anglo-French note. The reference to the League was to be modified (the Soviet government affected to fear that the machinery of the League was to be used to delay immediate assistance); the proposed clause that mutual assistance should not prejudice the rights and position of other powers was to be deleted (the object of this article was to prevent use of the territory of, say, Poland without Polish consent); the political agreement should come into force simultaneously with a military agreement. The British and French had no desire to expose their military position to the Russians until a political agreement was assured, and a new difficulty now arose in the unwillingness of the Baltic States and Holland to be guaranteed, lest a German attack should be provoked. Agreement was, however, near by the end of June, but on 4 July Molotov suddenly made explicit a demand that had been hinted at by Maisky in London on 9 May, and clearly foreshadowed by Molotov himself on 30 May, to the effect that mutual assistance should operate in the case of indirect as well as direct aggression. By indirect aggression was meant the internal disruption of a state (such as, for instance,

Hitler's use of Slovakia to destroy Czecho-Slovakia), and counter-action was to be taken by any signatory considering its security threatened. The proposal seemed to foreshadow possible Soviet military interference in countries such as the Baltic states, whose governments were more Russophobe than Germanophobe, and once more time was absorbed in the arduous search for a formula. But agreement was again at length almost reached, and according to Bonnet[1] a draft written on 24 July contained slight disagreement on one clause only. On 25 July Britain and France agreed to send military missions to Moscow.

In order to consult together on the way, the military missions travelled by sea and reached Moscow only on 11 August. By that date it was perfectly evident to the Soviet leaders that they could obtain an agreement with the Germans if they wanted to, and on 10 August the first major step towards definition of political issues had been taken in Berlin. In the military discussions Britain and France were forced to reveal their military weakness, which meant for the Soviet Union that even if a binding agreement were concluded, the western powers could do little to take the weight of the German attack from Soviet shoulders. On 14 August Voroshilov suddenly asked whether Soviet troops could enter Polish territory in order to be able to move against Germany, and said that if not further negotiations were useless. The British and French officers had no instructions on this political issue, and heavy pressure was brought on Warsaw by London and Paris; but the Poles refused to provoke, as they put it, a German attack by making a prior commitment to allow Soviet troops to pass through their territory should a German attack actually take place. On 21 August it was suddenly announced that Ribbentrop would shortly fly to Moscow, and on 23 August the Nazi-Soviet pact, dividing eastern Europe into spheres of influence between the two countries, was signed.

It is impossible on the evidence available to measure the extent to which British policy was responsible for the failure of the negotiations with the U.S.S.R. Certainly France was less unwilling to meet the successive Soviet demands than Britain and, in the light of rumours about Soviet-German negotiations, France pressed Britain to move faster. The decision to help the negotiations along by sending to Moscow a not very senior

[1] Bonnet, G., *Fin d'une Europe*, p. 201. Bourguin, 1948.

official in the person of William Strang, whereas Chamberlain himself had gone to Berchtesgaden and Ribbentrop was to go to Moscow, did not pass unnoticed in the Kremlin. The military missions were not headed by the British and French military chiefs, and therefore did not rank with Voroshilov who led the Russian delegation. Their journeying by sea suggested no very great sense of urgency. The Soviet suspicion that the British government was using the negotiations with themselves merely in order to obtain more favourable terms in an agreement with Germany was echoed in the British Press.[1] Chamberlain, presumably with the knowledge of the senior members of the government, was in fact still investigating the possibility of coming to terms with Germany. Evidence of this is to be found in the discussions between Sir Horace Wilson and von Dirksen, the German ambassador in London.[2] Rumours about these feelers could hardly have passed unnoticed in Moscow, particularly when information appeared in the Press in July about economic negotiations then being conducted between a German official and the Secretary for Overseas Trade, Mr. R. S. Hudson. Though the details of the information were inaccurate, and though the talks came to nothing, the fact that they were being held undoubtedly stimulated the Kremlin's customary distrust. There is nothing to support the view that Chamberlain was in fact trying to buy off the Germans at the expense of the U.S.S.R., nor indeed does it seem from the inconclusive nature of the Wilson-Dirksen talks that he now had much hope of reaching a settlement with Germany. It seems rather that he could not bring himself to end all contact with Berlin and thus exclude even the faint possibility that the building of the anti-aggression front might make Germany willing to listen to reason. If it was in fact this that persuaded him to keep the line to Berlin open, it was yet one more example of bad diplomatic technique; for Germany would certainly not be frightened unless and until the peace front was solid, and the fact of talking to Germany before agreement with the U.S.S.R. was reached itself made that agreement less likely.

---

[1] "In restating the readiness of the country to negotiate with Germany before the negotiations with Soviet Russia were completed, the Foreign Secretary ran a slight risk of being misunderstood in Moscow." *The Times*, 13 June 1939.

[2] *Documents and Materials Relating to the Eve of the Second World War*, Vol. II, pp. 67-197. Foreign Languages Publishing House, Moscow, 1948.

Nevertheless, when all this is said, it may well be that nothing that Britain could have done after March 1939 would have won the Soviet alliance. The roots of distrust, not merely from ideological prejudices, but also from past Anglo-French policies, had gone very deep; and once it became apparent that agreement with the Nazis was possible, that alternative inevitably became more alluring. It is probable that the men in the Politburo did not finally make up their minds until August, but as soon as the security afforded by the Anglo-French guarantees to Poland and Rumania was theirs, the logic of the situation worked in favour of the Nazis. But to say that the hesitant and somewhat equivocal conduct of Britain during the negotiations probably had no decisive effect on their outcome is not to deny the great importance of the Polish and Rumanian guarantees, or of the decision to drop the four-power declaration at Poland's behest and despite Soviet approval. The turning-point may well have been then; but it can only be surmised whether, even had matters been better judged at that time, the Soviet Union would not still have been persuaded to a German alliance when they discovered the extent of the western powers' military weakness.

While these parallel German-Soviet and Anglo-French-Soviet negotiations were in train, German-Polish relations grew neither easier nor more tense. On 28 April Hitler announced in the Reichstag the proposals he had made to Poland which would not again be "offered". At the same time he denounced the Polish-German non-aggression pact of 1934 and the Anglo-German naval treaty of 1935. On 5 May Beck made a firm public statement in reply. At this time Mussolini suddenly decided finally to throw in his lot with Germany, and the terms of an offensive and defensive alliance (subsequently known as the Pact of Steel) were agreed on 7 May and signed on the 22nd. To the agreement Mussolini appended a memorandum envisaging war not before 1942, but on the next day, while Ciano was still in Berlin, Hitler announced to his immediate political and military advisers his decision to attack Poland at the first suitable opportunity. On 19 May French and Polish officers agreed on a military convention which should be operative after certain modifications to the Franco-Polish alliance of 1921 had been made: these modifications were never agreed because the French desired their obligations to parallel those of Britain, and Britain was unwilling to sign the projected pact with Poland until agreement was reached with the U.S.S.R., so that there should be no conflict between the two. No formal staff talks therefore took place, and the alliance with Poland, which was preferred to that with the Soviet Union, was never fortified by a military understanding.

Early in August the situation in Danzig suddenly worsened, and the concentration of German troops in the east, ostensibly for the celebration of the battle of Tannenberg on 27 August, suggested that some action was imminent. Hitler expected that his agreement with Stalin would cause Britain and France to abandon Poland, and he attached little importance to a letter from Chamberlain on 23 August saying that the Nazi-Soviet pact would not affect Britain's obligations to Poland, but that he was ready to discuss matters if a peaceful atmosphere were restored. Hitler replied peremptorily that the Danzig situation had to be settled, and that he would mobilize if the military precautions of Britain and France continued. During the morning he gave the order for the attack on Poland to start at 4.40 a.m. on 26 August. He apparently decided, however, that a positive effort would have to be made by himself to detach Britain and France from Poland, so on 25 August he summoned to his presence first Henderson, and after him the French ambassador, Coulondre. To each he made bold and generous offers of lasting peace and a world settlement once the Polish issue was out of the way. But the old tale had been heard once too often even in London and Paris. On the 28th Henderson returned from London with the British reply that Poland and Germany should negotiate directly on the basis of Polish independence and under an international guarantee, but that general discussions and agreement were possible only if the Polish question were amicably settled. In the meantime Hitler had been given pause on 25 August, first by a message from Rome saying that Italy was not ready for war and large supplies of war materials were needed, and secondly by news from London of the signature of an Anglo-Polish treaty of mutual assistance. He accordingly cancelled his order for the attack on Poland. After some further meaningless diplomatic convolutions, however, the order was renewed at 12.40 p.m. on 31 August for the attack to begin at 4.45 a.m. on 1 September, and this time the armies and

the aircraft were not held back. At midday on the 31st the
Italians in a last despairing effort came up with proposals for a
conference. Bonnet promised to wait until midday on 3 September for the German reply, which the Germans delayed until noon
on the 2nd. But in London a spark of fire had at long last been
struck, and Halifax refused to enter a conference unless the
German forces withdrew from Poland. Mussolini would not
even propose such a condition to Hitler: Bonnet, game to the
last, then suggested that the Germans should make a symbolic
withdrawal, a proposal that Ciano threw into the wastepaper
basket.[1] Halifax pressed Bonnet for an early ultimatum, but
Bonnet insisted on waiting until noon on the 3rd as he had
promised to Ciano. Chamberlain in the House on the evening of
the 2nd had a hostile reception when he had no news of a British
ultimatum, now already two days after the German attack on
Poland had been launched; and later that night Halifax told
the French ambassador in London that a declaration of war
would be made by Britain the next morning. Bonnet, however,
stood firm. The British ultimatum was accordingly delivered by
Henderson at 9 a.m. to expire at 11 a.m., and the French ultimatum was delivered at noon to expire at 5 p.m. Among the
reasons for Daladier's agreement to Bonnet's shilly-shallying
was the desire to carry French mobilization as far as possible
before the actual declaration of war, while Britain on the other
hand as a primarily naval power wished for an early declaration
so that a naval blockade could be put into effect. But the British
and French failure to synchronize their declarations of war was
typical of the whole course of their relations between the two
world wars: minor divergencies of policy or outlook had been
permitted so to dominate the ultimate identity of their interests
and aspirations that one was now left powerless to resist the
resurgent might of Germany, and the other was to be brought
to the very brink of ruin.[2]

---

[1] *Ciano's Diary, 1939-43*, p. 143. Heinemann, 1947.
[2] By far the best and most complete account of these last stages of inter-war
diplomacy is to be found in Namier, L. B., *Diplomatic Prelude, 1938-1939*.

Chapter 13

CONCLUSION

THE EVIDENCE of the Nuremberg trials and of the German Foreign Office documents now being published has conclusively proved the deliberate intention and plan of Hitler and a few of his leading coadjutors to start a second world war. Hitler's lust for power was such that it could find fulfilment only in the suffering and death of millions of his fellow-men; and the exaltation in the Nazi philosophy of force, of racial supremacy and of the *Führer-prinzip* meant that the addicts of Nazism also could find satisfaction only in a new and greater conflict. The Nazi minority appealed skilfully to deep yearnings in the German soul, played adroitly on the "injustices" of the Versailles treaty, and swept to power on the wave of fear, distrust and intrigue thrown up in Germany by the effects of the World Economic Crisis.

Similarly in Japan a small group of military extremists, dreaming of domination of China and the Far East, and thence of the world, planned to enforce their will by fire and the sword. Held in check by the victory of democracy in the First World War and by the successful administration of the Minseito governments in the 1920s, they too were able to break loose from the restraining grasp of more cautious hands by reason of the misery and depression that engulfed Japan in 1930 and 1931. With no ties of sympathy or understanding between them the Japanese and the Nazis were yet able to make common cause in the endeavour to destroy a mutual enemy.

Behind these, and little like them, trailed the Italian *Duce*. His vice was less lust than vanity; the scorn and triumph of his German associate held for him a fascination like that of the snake for the rabbit; and he whipped his rancour against Britain and France to a point where he could no longer resist dragging his cowed but unwilling people in the wake of the Nazi destroyer. In the hatred, the pride and the vanity of these men, and in the political, economic and social conditions in which they could prosper, is to be found the cause of the Second World War, and they have paid, though not in full, for the evil that they wrought.

But the Second World War could as well have been prevented had not the legatees of the Christian tradition been consumed by pleasure-seeking, by selfishness or by apathy. In the United States the wave of fraternal idealism of the latter part of the First World War was swamped in the rush to get the boys home, in the disillusionments of the peace, and in the party wrangles between the Wilsonians and the isolationists. The poise and assurance of France had perished with the flower of her youth in the trenches, and she no longer had the power, and soon not the spirit, to sustain the burdens of European leadership which her great tradition and her recent victory laid upon her. In Britain the overmastering desire to avoid being once more drawn into a European or world conflict succeeded in repressing the sneaking conviction that never again could Britain hold the balance of European destiny in the way that her nineteenth-century wealth and maritime power had enabled her to do. From the union of this yearning to keep out and the fear that it was no longer possible sprang the compromises, the confusions and the aspirations that have been described in the preceding pages.

The balance of power that Britain had sought to maintain in Europe could continue after the mighty achievements of Bismarck in the third quarter of the nineteenth century only through an effective alliance of France and Russia. In that counterpoise Britain's weight might well have seemed decisive. But the foundations of that balance were destroyed by the Bolshevik revolution in Russia, and by the economic and demographic weakness of a France laid waste by the ravages of war; and the statesmen and people of Britain failed to see that the shadow of French dominance in Europe but masked the reality of German power. In fighting that shadow, in refusing to throw her weight into the European scale to replace that of Russia, Britain ensured that French policy took such a form that the reassertion of German power when it came drew its inspiration from the most unrational and barbaric strands in German culture. Britain moreover attempted to play this part of restoring the balance in Europe, and of herself mediating between the two sides, at a time when her own power and resources were no longer of decisive weight. Necessarily in some degree sensible of this loss of strength, Britain's leaders endeavoured to associate their country far more closely than hitherto with the Dominions and, until the time of Neville Chamberlain, with the United States; but the interests both of the Dominions and of America were not judged to require the maintenance of any particular order in Europe, with the consequence that Britain's nostalgia for her part of European arbitrator was greatly stimulated. When at length the error of this course was discovered, it was too late to prevent the brutal onslaught of the Nazis, and all but too late to recover from their blows even with the powerful sustainment of the United States.

This same tradition of British policy powerfully influenced her attitude to the League of Nations. When the American mother abandoned her child, the father of the League perforce took a new wife whose ideas about the infant's upbringing and career were very different from his own. He wished the League to serve as a more effective instrument in his tried and trusted policies of mediation and conciliation, but his new French partner saw the organization at Geneva as a means of hindering any new German attempt to master the continent of Europe. To most leaders in Britain those organs of the League and those clauses in the Covenant were deemed most important which looked towards the conciliation of disputes, the peaceful revision of international arrangements, and the removal or reduction of social or economic causes of conflict. To most Frenchmen the League was far more a policeman who should swiftly act to prevent crimes against the peace by the German prisoner recently released on parole. This difference of view about the League as conciliator or as policeman reflected the different needs and aspirations of Britain and France; but it also mirrored the unreconciled duality of function given to the League by the authors of the Covenant. To this duality was added an allied but not precisely similar divergence of opinion; whether the League should number among its members as many states in the world as possible, or whether it should include only members of a certain outlook and state of development. The former universalist view meant that unity for coercive action was much more difficult to achieve, but that scope for conciliation or the amelioration of causes of conflict would be greater: moreover it reflected the fact that technologically, economically and strategically the world was now a unit. The latter view made more probable effective action in a particular region, and it reflected the fact that politically, socially and culturally the world was far from unified. Britain as a world power with world interests and practised in the arts of conciliation naturally inclined to the universalist view with limited coercive responsibilities; and when eventually under domestic pressure her government invoked the coercive provisions of the Covenant, it was in an area of no vital economic or strategic importance. France, whose fears, though not altogether her interests, were centred in Europe, laid more emphasis on the coercive aspects of the Covenant, with the intention that they should be ignored outside Europe. The United States, understandably even less aware of the realities of twentieth-century international relationships, thought by political action to insulate herself from world conflicts despite her close economic links with other continents, in the mistaken belief that strategically she could make herself immune from attack. Each of the three powers thus contributed to the disaster of 1939, while the failure of the League may be ultimately ascribed to the fact that the world was in some senses a unit, in others not, and the policies of the major states of the world, and the terms of the Covenant itself, reflected that confusion.

The failure of British policy in the inter-war years resulted from two fundamental errors—the attempt to pursue traditional policies when British power was no longer sufficient and world conditions were no longer wholly suitable, and the pursuit of conciliation and tolerance to the point of failure to recognize evil, and in evil danger. British power could no longer be decisive in every dispute that might arise in almost any part of the world. World conditions were now such that Britain was bound up with events in Europe, but at the same time she could not ignore the views and policies of the Dominions and those of the United States. Britain's continued existence as a world power depends upon her reconciliation of these three complementary interests, but her influence will count for little if her statesmen still fail to recognize that pursuit of the expedient to the exclusion of the just may in the end prove the most impolitic.

BIBLIOGRAPHY

THIS small selected bibliography is not confined to British foreign policy but covers the inter-war years as a whole. All titles are published in Britain except where otherwise stated.

1. GENERAL SURVEYS

GATHORNE-HARDY, G. M., *A Short History of International Affairs 1920-1939*. 4th Ed. Oxford University Press, 1950.
> The best general survey of the period, but does not take into account recent documentary evidence.

BAUMONT, M., *La Faillite de la Paix 1918-1939*. 2nd Ed. Paris, Presses Universitaires de France, 1945.
> The best general text-book in French.

TOYNBEE, A. J. (ed.), *Survey of International Affairs*. Oxford University Press. Annually.
> Annual publications written a few years after the period to which they refer and still of great value.

MANSERGH, N., *Survey of British Commonwealth Affairs*. Oxford University Press, 1952.
> A full and penetrating survey of foreign policies within the Commonwealth between 1931 and 1939.

CHURCHILL, W. S., *The Second World War*, Vol. I, "The Gathering Storm". Cassell, 1948.
> Bold and broad survey in characteristic Churchillian prose.

The History of the Times, Vol. IV, "The 150th Anniversary and Beyond". Printing House Square, 1952.
> Startlingly frank and very informative account of the history and influence of Britain's leading newspaper.

2. MAJOR DOCUMENTARY SOURCES

WODDWARD, E. L. and BUTLER, R. (eds.), *Documents on British Foreign Policy 1919-1939*. H.M.S.O. Progress.
> So far published: Series I, Vols. I—IV (1919-20)
> Series II, Vols. I—IV (1930-3)
> Series III, Vols. I—VI (1938-9)

Bibliography

Documents on German Foreign Policy, 1918-1945. H.M.S.O. Progress. So far published: Series D, Vols. I-IV (1936-9)

Papers Relating to the Foreign Relations of the United States. Department of State, Washington. Progress. So far published: Vols. 1919-35.

LEAGUE OF NATIONS *Official Journal.*

Proceedings of the International Military Tribunal at Nuremberg. H.M.S.O., 1946-9.

MUGGERIDGE, M. (ed.), *Ciano's Diplomatic Papers.* Odhams, 1948.

WHEELER-BENNETT, J. W. (ed.), *Documents on International Affairs.* Oxford University Press. Annually.

DEGRAS, JANE (ed.), *Soviet Documents on Foreign Policy*, Vols. I-II 1917-32. Oxford University Press, 1951-2.

Documents and Materials Relating to the Eve of the Second World War. 2 Vols. Moscow, Foreign Languages Publishing House, 1948.

3. MEMOIRS, BIOGRAPHIES AND MONOGRAPHS

A. EUROPE

BARUCH, B. M., *The Making of the Reparation and Economic Sections of the Treaty.* New York, Harper, 1920.
   Account by a member of the United States delegation.

BASCH, A., *The Danube Basin and the German Economic Sphere.* New York, Columbia University Press, 1944.
   Clear survey of German economic expansion in south-east Europe.

BIRDSALL, P., *Versailles Twenty Years After.* Allen and Unwin, 1941.
   Dispassionate survey of 1919 peacemaking.

BONNET, G., *Défense de la Paix.* 2 Vols. Genève, Bourguin, 1946-8.
   Skilful but highly tendentious apologia by the chief French appeaser.

BRENAN, G., *Spanish Labyrinth.* 2nd Ed. Cambridge University Press, 1950.
   Interesting sociological account of Spain before 1936.

BULLOCK, A., *Hitler, a Study in Tyranny.* Odhams, 1952.
   Brilliant and authoritative account of the life of the German dictator.

CAMERON, E. R., *Prologue to Appeasement.* Washington, American Council on Public Affairs, 1942.
   A good doctoral thesis on the evolution of French policy and parties 1933-6.

CARTER, G. M., *The British Commonwealth and International Security.* Toronto, Ryerson Press, 1947.
   A careful and documented account.

CHAPUT, R. A., *Disarmament in British Foreign Policy*. Allen and Unwin, 1935.
> A full and detailed account of the British attitude to problems of disarmament on land, on sea, and in the air.

CIANO, G., *Diary 1937-1938*. Methuen, 1952.
> Contains much useful information.

COULONDRE, R., *De Staline à Hitler*. Paris, Hachette, 1950.
> Informative account of the former French ambassador in Moscow and Berlin.

CREMONA, P., and MACARTNEY, M. H. H., *Italy's Foreign and Colonial Policy 1914-1937*. Oxford University Press, 1938.
> Clear account.

ESCH, P. A. M. VAN DER, *Prelude to War*. The Hague, Martinus Nijhoff, 1951.
> Studious account of the international repercussions of the Spanish Civil War.

FEILING, K., *The Life of Neville Chamberlain*. Macmillan, 1946.
> Ill-written semi-apologia for Chamberlain, but some private documentary material.

FLANDIN, P.-E., *Politique Française, 1919-1940*. Paris, Editions Nouvelles, 1947.
> Apologia of the former French Prime Minister and Foreign Minister.

FRANÇOIS-PONCET, A., *Souvenirs d'une Ambassade à Berlin*. Paris, Flammarion, 1946.
> Informative memoirs of the former French ambassador in Berlin and Rome.

GAFENCU, G., *The Last Days of Europe*. Muller, 1947.
> Account by the former Rumanian Foreign Minister with some valuable material.

HENDERSON, SIR N., *Failure of a Mission*. Hodder and Stoughton, 1940.
> Little reliance should be placed on these memoirs of the former British ambassador in Berlin.

JORDAN, W. M., *Great Britain, France and the German Problem*. Oxford University Press, 1943.
> Scholarly and documented study of the problems of reparations, security and disarmament. One of the best monographs on the period.

KEYNES, J. M., *The Economic Consequences of the Peace*. Macmillan, 1919.
> Brilliant controversial analysis of the economic clauses of Versailles.

Bibliography

MACARTNEY, C. A., *Hungary and Her Successors*. Oxford University Press, 1937.
Good account of the countries of the Danube Basin in the inter-war period.

MACFADYEAN, A., *Reparations Reviewed*. Benn, 1930.
The best general survey of the reparations problem.

MANTOUX, E., *The Carthaginian Peace*. Oxford University Press, 1946.
Written as an answer to Keynes. Better on political than economic aspects.

MARSTON, F. S., *The Peace Conference of 1919*. Oxford University Press, 1944.
Scholarly analysis of the machinery of the Paris peace conference.

MASON, J. B., *The Danzig Dilemma*. California, Stanford University Press, 1946.
Repetitive but authoritative history of the Free City.

McCALLUM, R. B., *Public Opinion and the Last Peace*. Oxford University Press, 1944.
Penetrating and provocative survey of the development of British attitudes to Versailles.

MONROE, E., *The Mediterranean in Politics*. Oxford University Press, 1938.
Stimulating study of the interests of the powers in the Mediterranean.

MORGAN, BRIG. GEN. J. H., *Assize of Arms*. Methuen, 1945.
First-hand account of German evasion of the disarmament clauses of Versailles.

NAMIER, L. B., *Diplomatic Prelude 1938-1939*. Macmillan, 1948.
Masterly analysis of the immediate pre-war period. Now somewhat dated, but of permanent value as an example of method.

NOËL, L., *L'agression allemande contre la Pologne*. Paris, Flammarion, 1946.
Very informative account of the former French ambassador in Warsaw.

PADELFORD, N. J., *International Law and Diplomacy in the Spanish Civil Strife*. New York, Macmillan, 1939.
Painstaking study of the implications of the Spanish Civil War for International Law.

PETRIE, SIR CHARLES, *The Life and Letters of the Right Hon. Sir Austen Chamberlain*, Vol. II. Cassell, 1940.
Much information in this standard life.

RAPHAËL, G., *Allemagne et Pologne*. Paris, Delagrave, 1932.
Excellent study of Polish-German relations.

Rossi, A., *The Russo-German Alliance, 1939-1941*. Chapman and Hall, 1950.

Anti-Soviet, but useful account of the Nazi-Soviet pact of 1939-41.

Seton-Watson, H., *Eastern Europe Between the Wars, 1918-1941*. Cambridge University Press, 1945.

Excellent survey of the problems of eastern European countries in the inter-war period.

Seton-Watson, R. W., *Britain and the Dictators*. Cambridge University Press, 1938.

Now somewhat dated, but a still useful account of British relations with the U.S.S.R., Italy and Germany.

Schmidt, Dr. P., *Hitler's Interpreter*. Heinemann, 1951.

Less information than might be expected from the sole witness of many of Hitler's interviews.

Simon, Viscount, *Retrospect*. Hutchinson, 1952.

Revealing memoirs of the former Foreign Secretary and Lord Chancellor.

Sutton, Eric (ed.), *Gustav Stresemann: His Diaries, Letters and Papers*. 3 Vols. Macmillan, 1935-40.

Essential to an understanding of Germany's foreign policy in the 1920s.

Temperley, H. W. C. (ed.), *History of the Peace Conference of Paris*. 6 Vols. Oxford University Press, 1920-4.

The standard account.

Toynbee, A. J., *The World after the Peace Conference*. Oxford University Press, 1925.

Survey of the world in 1919 written with Professor Toynbee's customary penetration and lucidity.

Webster, Sir Charles K. and others, *United Kingdom Policy, Foreign, Strategic and Economic*. R.I.I.A., 1950.

Three essays by experts on British foreign, strategic and economic policy.

Wheeler-Bennett, J. W., *Munich, Prologue to Tragedy*. Macmillan, 1948.

A good account of the Czech crisis, but not a definitive work.

Wiskemann, E., *Czechs and Germans*. Oxford University Press, 1938.

Excellent study of the problems of Czech-German relations.

Wiskemann, E., *The Rome-Berlin Axis*. Oxford University Press, 1949.

Lively and documented study of the Axis. Another of the best monographs on the period.

WOLFERS, A., *Britain and France Between two Wars*. New York, Harcourt, Brace & Co., 1940.
Very clear survey, with some material supplementary to Jordan.

B. THE SOVIET UNION

BELOFF, M., *The Foreign Policy of Soviet Russia, 1929-1941*. 2 Vols. Oxford University Press, 1947-9.
Standard account.

BORKENAU, F., *The Communist International*. Faber, 1938.
Brilliant and acid history by ex-Communist.

CARR, E. H., *A History of the Soviet Union*. Macmillan. Progress. Vols. I-III, "The Bolshevik Revolution, 1917-1923."
Written with Mr. Carr's customary incisive and logical analysis.

CHAMBERLIN, W. H., *The Russian Revolution*. 2 Vols. New York, Macmillan, 1935.
A fair and unbiased account.

COATES, W. P. and Z. K., *A History of Anglo-Soviet Relations*. Lawrence and Wishart, 1943.
An account by two well-known Soviet apologists.

DAVIES, J. E., *Mission to Moscow*. Gollancz, 1944.
Informative but slightly unreliable memoirs of the former United States ambassador in Moscow.

DEUTSCHER, I., *Stalin, a Political Biography*. 2nd Imp., Oxford University Press, 1950.
Powerful and convincing study.

FISCHER, L., *The Soviets in World Affairs*. 2 Vols. Cape, 1930.
Much documentary material in informative survey.

FISCHER, R., *Stalin and German Communism*. Oxford University Press, 1948.
Penetrating though unreliable analysis by ex-Communist.

ROSENBERG, A., *A History of Bolshevism*. Oxford University Press, 1934.
Clear and comparatively objective account by ex-Communist.

TARACOUZIO, T. A., *War and Peace in Soviet Diplomacy*. New York, Macmillan, 1940.
Legalistic and formal, but valuable study of the significance of war and peace for the Soviet Union.

TOWSTER, J., *Political Power in the U.S.S.R.* Oxford University Press, 1948.
Full and informative study of the forms and reality of Soviet government.

C. THE MIDDLE EAST

ANTONIUS, G., *The Arab Awakening.* Hamilton, 1938.
> Pro-Arab account of Arab nationalism.

BULLARD, SIR R., *Britain and the Middle East.* Hutchinson, 1951.
> Swift and shrewd survey by a former ambassador in Teheran.

KIRK, G., *A Short History of the Middle East.* Methuen, 1948.
> Clear survey.

KNATCHBULL-HUGESSEN, SIR HUGHE, *Diplomat in Peace and War.* Murray, 1949.
> Memoirs of the able former ambassador in Turkey.

Royal Institute of International Affairs Information Paper No. 20: *Great Britain and Palestine, 1915-1945.* R.I.I.A., 1946.
> Short survey of the Palestine problem.

Royal Institute of International Affairs: *The Middle East.* R.I.I.A., 1950.
> A careful and comprehensive survey.

SHOTWELL, J. T., and DEAK, F., *Turkey at the Straits.* New York, Macmillan, 1940.
> A classic short analysis.

WEIZMANN, CHAIM, *Trial and Error.* Hamilton, 1949.
> Autobiography of the greatest of the Zionists.

D. THE FAR EAST

BASSETT, R., *Democracy and Foreign Policy.* Longmans, 1952.
> A full but rather tendentious study of public opinion in the Manchurian crisis.

BORG, D., *American Policy and the Chinese Revolution, 1925-1928.* New York, Macmillan, 1947.
> Careful and documented account.

HUBBARD, G. E., *British Far Eastern Policy.* New York, Institute of Pacific Relations, 1943.
> An account of British policy in the Far East from 1834 to 1939.

HUDSON, G. F., *The Far East in World Politics.* Oxford University Press, 1937.
> Excellent and clear survey of the international politics of the Far East.

PRATT, J. T., *War and Politics in China.* Cape, 1943.
> Much good material presented by a former member of the Foreign Service.

RENOUVIN, P., *La Question d'Extrême Orient.* Paris, Hachette, 1946.
> Covers much the same ground as Hudson, with additional consideration of economic factors.

Bibliography

Royal Institute of International Affairs Information Paper No. 21(*a*): *China and Japan*. R.I.I.A., 1938.
  Clear and concise survey.

SMITH, S. R., *The Manchurian Crisis, 1931-1932*. New York, Columbia University Press, 1948.
  Anti-Stimson bias, but nevertheless excellent study, well-documented and scholarly.

STIMSON, H. L., *The Far Eastern Crisis*. Harper, 1936.
  Slightly disingenuous account by the U.S. Secretary of State at the time of Manchuria.

WILLOUGHBY, W. W., *The Sino-Japanese Controversy and the League*. Baltimore, John Hopkins, 1935.
  Painstaking account of the Manchurian crisis and the League of Nations.

E. THE UNITED STATES

BAILEY, T. A., *A Diplomatic History of the American People*. 3rd Ed. New York, Crofts, 1947.
  Rather superficial Republican survey.

BISSON, T. A., *American Policy in the Far East, 1931-1940*. New York, Macmillan, 1945.
  Concise survey with some useful material.

FLEMING, D. F., *The United States and the League of Nations, 1918-1920*. New York, Putnams, 1932.
  Full, pro-Wilson account of the defeat of the Covenant in the United States.

FLEMING, D. F., *The United States and World Organization, 1920-1933*. New York, Columbia University Press, 1938.
  Less valuable continuation of the former work.

GREW, JOSEPH C., *Turbulent Era*. Hammond, 1953.
  Much valuable first-hand information in this life of a leading career diplomat of the United States.

HULL, C., *The Memoirs of Cordell Hull*. 2 Vols. New York, Macmillan, 1948.
  Rather dull and complacent, but contains some material.

LANGER, W. L., and GLEASON, S. EVERETT, *The Challenge to Isolation*. Royal Institute of International Affairs, 1952.
  The first of two volumes giving a scholarly and documented account of the diplomatic emergence of the United States, 1937-41.

NEVINS, A., *America in World Affairs*. Oxford University Press, 1941.
  Slight but suggestive survey.

F. THE WORLD ECONOMIC CRISIS

ARNDT, H. W., *Economic Lessons of the 1930s*. Royal Institute of International Affairs, 1944.
Brilliant but slightly tendentious analysis of economic policies in the 'thirties.

HODSON, H. V., *Slump and Recovery, 1929-1937*. Oxford University Press, 1938.
Valuable survey of the course of the economic crisis.

League of Nations, *Causes and Phases of the World Depression*. A.22: 1931:IIa.
Valuable contemporary view of the crisis.

ROBBINS, L., *The Great Depression*. Macmillan, 1934.
An economic analysis of the crisis.

G. THE LEAGUE OF NATIONS

GREAVES, H. R. G., *The League Committees and World Order*. Oxford University Press, 1931.
Conscientious factual account of the non-political activities of the League.

MILLER, D. H., *The Drafting of the Covenant*. 2 Vols. Putnams, 1928.
Account of the origins of the Covenant by Wilson's legal adviser.

NOEL-BAKER, P. J., *The Geneva Protocol*. King, 1925.
Account of the Protocol by a leading British Socialist.

WALTERS, F. P., *A History of the League of Nations*. 2 Vols. Oxford University Press, 1952.
The former Deputy Secretary-General of the League has here written what is likely long to remain the standard history.

WEBSTER, C. K. and HERBERT, S., *The League of Nations in Theory and Practice*. Allen & Unwin, 1933.
Short, clear survey of the League to 1933.

ZIMMERN, SIR ALFRED, *The League of Nations and the Rule of Law, 1918-1935*. Macmillan, 1936.
Valuable analysis by a life-long protagonist of international order.

INDEX

Index